THE FIRST DAY AT GETTYSBURG

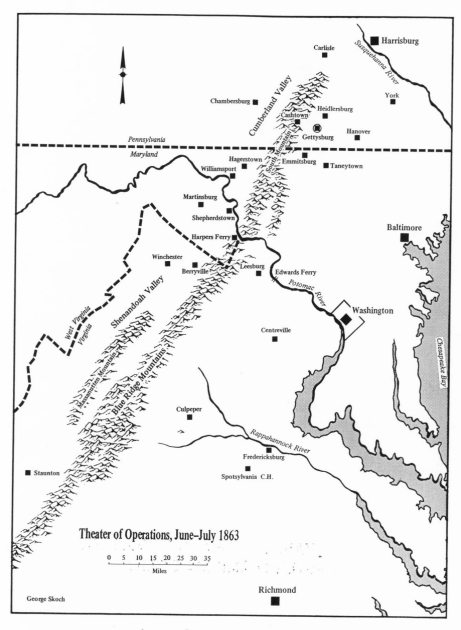

Theater of Operations, June–July 1863

THE FIRST DAY AT GETTYSBURG

Essays on Confederate and Union Leadership

EDITED BY

Gary W. Gallagher

THE KENT STATE UNIVERSITY PRESS
Kent, Ohio, and London, England

© 1992 by The Kent State University Press, Kent, Ohio 44242
Library of Congress Catalog Card Number 91-31379
ISBN 0-87338-456-3
ISBN 0-87338-457-1 (pbk.)
Manufactured in the United States of America

Library of Congress Cataloging–in–Publication Data

The First day at Gettysburg : essays on Confederate and Union
leadership / edited by Gary W. Gallagher.
p.   cm.
Includes bibliographical references (p.   ) and index.
ISBN 0-87338-456-3 (cloth :   alk.) ∞ — ISBN 0-87338-457-1
(pbk. :   alk.) ∞
1. Gettysburg (Pa.), Battle of, 1863.   2. Command of troops—Case
studies.   I. Gallagher, Gary W.
E475.53.F57   1992
973.7'349—dc20   91-31379

British Library Cataloging-in-Publication data are available.

Contents

Introduction

GARY W. GALLAGHER

The literature on the Battle of Gettysburg dwarfs that devoted to any other military operation in American history. Vast in scope and horrible in human cost, the battle serves as a decisive watershed in the popular imagination—before the three days of brutal combat on July 1–3, 1863, a Confederate tide swept forward. Following the sharp defeat in Pennsylvania, Southern will and resources slowly drained away. Four and one-half months after the Army of Northern Virginia retreated from the battlefield, Abraham Lincoln seemingly confirmed Gettysburg's preeminence when he dedicated a national cemetery on ground where the Union army had anchored its defense. Speaking of the Northern men who had fought at Gettysburg, Lincoln prophesied that the world "can never forget what they did here." Americans have not forgotten, displaying a persistent interest in new accounts of the campaign and visiting the battlefield, now the centerpiece of the National Park Service's Civil War holdings, in large numbers.

Military historians frequently criticize the popular attention accorded Gettysburg. They see Vicksburg as equally important and the autumn campaigning of 1862 as perhaps more decisive in deciding the fate of the Union. Yet even the most skeptical student scarcely can deny that Gettysburg represented a turning point for both armies. On the Confederate side, soldiers and officers conditioned to expect victories under R. E. Lee's leadership faced the specter of failure. Brigadier General Stephen Dodson Ramseur of North Carolina typified this phenomenon. Supremely confident as Lee's troops marched north, Ramseur assured his wife on June 23, 1863, that the army expected "to make a bold and successful campaign." A month after the battle, a chastened Ramseur conceded that "our

great campaign, admirably planned & more admirably executed up to the fatal days at Gettysburg, has failed. Which I
was not prepared to anticipate." For many Federal soldiers,
Gettysburg ended a dreary cycle of reverses during which feelings of inferiority had mingled with a sense that timid generals
denied them a chance to test their mettle against the Confederates. Robert G. Carter of Massachusetts captured these atti-
tudes in a letter to his father on July 14, 1863: "We went into
the bloody battle of Gettysburg feeling that we had suffered too
much for the wretches, not to give them a *licking*, and we
fought like *devils.* . . . [We] fought one of the most terrible
battles on record and *whipped*—GLORY!!! *and chased them
by thunder!!!!*"

The outcome of Gettysburg depended to a significant degree
on leadership in the respective armies. Many writers have
asked, How did Lee lose the battle? Mythmakers of the Lost
Cause expended a great deal of energy in attempts to prove Lee
blameless in the defeat. With Jubal A. Early as its most vocal
exponent, this group cast "Jeb" Stuart, Richard S. Ewell, A. P.
Hill, and, most notably, James Longstreet as villains in a drama
featuring Lee as a frustrated genius unable to extract accept-
able performances from his subordinates. The spiritual descen-
dants of Early have continued to ignore Lee's own honest
acceptance of responsibility for the disaster of Gettysburg,
while their modern opponents take Lee at his word and largely
absolve his lieutenants. Still others resent accounts of the
battle that explain its outcome as a result of Confederate failures. The Army of the Potomac won the battle, they insist,
at least as much as the Army of Northern Virginia lost it.
Why not focus on Federal leadership in seeking reasons for
Northern victory?

Successive generations of historians have not exhausted the
subject of leadership at Gettysburg. This is especially true of
the first day's fighting, which has been the least studied portion of the battle. Although overshadowed by more famous action at the Peach Orchard, the Wheat Field, Devil's Den, and
Little Round Top on July 2 and the climactic assault against
Cemetery Ridge on July 3, the initial phase of the battle offers

historians the most interesting problems of leadership. The first day began as a meeting engagement and escalated into a full-scale battle, presenting a fluid environment charged with opportunity and potential disaster. The initiative lay with the Confederates, who benefited from superior numbers and serendipitous positioning of successive divisions as they arrived on the field. By the end of the day, Lee and his soldiers had won a major tactical victory. Should they have accomplished more? If so, who was responsible for their inability to do so? Could better Federal leadership have limited Confederate gains? These and other questions offer fruitful avenues of approach to the fighting on July 1.

The contributors to this book examine controversial aspects of leadership on the opening day at Gettysburg. The first and second essays concentrate on the Southern high command, evaluating Lee's strategy and tactics and the performances of Richard S. Ewell and A. P. Hill. Gettysburg marked the inaugural trial for the army's three-corps structure instituted following the death of "Stonewall" Jackson; it witnessed as well the debut in corps command of Ewell and Hill, who suffer invidious comparisons with Jackson in much of the literature on Gettysburg. The third essay shifts the spotlight to O. O. Howard and the officers of the Federal Eleventh Corps. Maligned at the time and usually cast as second-rate soldiers thereafter, Howard and his subordinates played a crucial part in the collapse of Northern resistance about midafternoon on July 1. Three notable debacles among Lee's brigadiers are the subject of the final essay. Sour notes in an apparent symphony of Confederate success, they foreshadowed weakness at this level of leadership that would haunt Lee during the campaigning of 1864.

These four essays join a literature on Gettysburg that runs to thousands of titles. The authors entered such extensively mined historical territory with trepidation, knowing that the first response to a new book on the campaign might be a jaded, Why bother? They hope that the essays, which together draw on sources ranging from the most accessible to the arcane, will give readers a useful combination of interpretation and fresh evidence. If the essays do no more than prompt further discussion, they will be counted a success.

This book grew out of papers given in June 1990 at the fourth annual conference on the Civil War at the Mont Alto Campus of Pennsylvania State University. As always, the opportunity to spend several days with able scholars and good friends proved delightful. The ready cooperation of Will Greene, Bob Krick, and Alan Nolan made publication of this book possible. Eileen Anne Gallagher once again helped prepare the manuscript, though she made clear her disapproval of passages at odds with her own interpretations. I cannot imagine better company with whom to work.

R. E. Lee and
July 1 at Gettysburg

ALAN T. NOLAN

lthough President Jefferson Davis approved of the Army of Northern Virginia's moving into Maryland and Pennsylvania in 1863, the Gettysburg campaign was General Robert E. Lee's idea. In 1914, Douglas Southall Freeman wrote that Lee's "army . . . had been wrecked at Gettysburg."[1] This catastrophic consequence was the result of leadership failures on the part of the army commander. The first of these was strategic; the second involved a series of errors in the execution of the campaign.

In regard to strategy, it is apparent that the drama of Gettysburg and the celebrated controversies associated with the battle have obscured the primary question about the campaign: Should it have been undertaken; should Lee have been in Pennsylvania in 1863? When questioning Lee's campaigns and battles, one is frequently confronted with the assertion that he had no alternative. Accordingly, before addressing the question of the wisdom of Lee's raid into Pennsylvania, one must consider whether he had an alternative.

On the eve of the campaign, during the period following Chancellorsville, Lee's army remained near Fredericksburg on the Rappahannock facing Joseph Hooker's Army of the Potomac, located on the north side of that river. In this situation, Lee had at least three possible options: to attack Hooker across the river, which surely would have been problematical, to assume the defensive as he had at Fredericksburg in December 1862 and was to do again in 1864; or to undertake a raid into the North. The most likely of these choices was surely the middle course—to assume the defensive and force the Army of the Potomac to come after him. Lee apologists, committed to the "no alternative" thesis, would exorcise this option. The analysis of Colonel Charles Marshall, Lee's aide-de-camp and military secretary, is illustrative. In an effort to justify the campaign, Marshall carefully constructed the no alternative argument. He identified the same three choices for Lee set forth above. Rejecting the choice of Lee's attacking across the river, he eliminated the defensive option by the naked assertion that had Lee stood on the defensive south of the river he "was bound to assume . . . the enemy would abandon his effort to dislodge him from his position at Fredericksburg, and would move his army to Richmond by water." This, Marshall insisted, would have required Lee to retreat to defend Richmond. Based on this assumption, Marshall eliminated the defensive option and, as if by magic, concluded that there was no alternative to the Gettysburg raid. That the Federals would not have moved against Lee but would, instead, have proceeded directly to Richmond by water is simply Marshall's hypothesis. In fact, the evidence since the 1862 withdrawal from the Peninsula pointed to the North's commitment to the overland route.[2]

The Southern army's need for food is the premise of another no alternative justification for Lee's moving into Maryland and Pennsylvania. The South's supply problems were severe, as Robert K. Krick has graphically stated.[3] Collecting supplies and living off the Northern country was surely a motive for the campaign. But the Army of Northern Virginia was sustained in Virginia from July 1863 until April 1865, so it was not necessary to go North for food and forage. If supplying the army had really been the motive for the campaign, a raid by small, mobile forces rather than the entire army would have had considerably more promise and less risk.

Since there was an alternative, we may return to the primary question: Should Lee have undertaken the campaign at all? This question cannot be meaningfully considered in the abstract. It must be considered within the context of the larger question of the appropriate grand strategy of the war from the standpoint of the Confederacy. In this larger respect, the concern is not military strategy in the sense of a campaign or

General Robert E. Lee.
(Courtesy of the Library of Congress)

battle, that is, operational strategy. Rather, it is grand strategy, that is, to paraphrase Carl von Clausewitz, the art of employing military forces to attain the objects of war, to support the national policy of the government that raises the military forces. In evaluating a general's performance, the only significant inquiry is whether the general's actions related positively or negatively to the war objective and national policy of his government.

The statements of two Confederate leaders describe quite different theories of the South's grand strategy to win the war: E. Porter Alexander, chief of ordnance of the Army of Northern Virginia and later chief of artillery of Longstreet's First Corps, has described the South's appropriate grand strategy in this way:

> When the South entered upon war with a power so immensely her superior in men & money, & all the wealth of modern resources in machinery and transportation appliances by land & sea, she could entertain but one single hope of final success. That was, that the desperation of her resistance would finally exact from her adversary such a price in blood & treasure as to exhaust the enthusiasm of its population for the objects of the war. We could not hope to *conquer* her. Our one chance was to wear her out.[4]

This fairly describes a defensive grand stategy—to wear the North out instead of trying to defeat the North militarily.

The second view was Lee's. It may be found in two letters to President Davis. The first, written en route to Gettysburg, is dated June 25, 1863, at Williamsport, Maryland. Lee states: "It seems to me that we cannot afford to keep our troops awaiting possible movements of the enemy, but that our true policy is, as far as we can, so to employ our own forces as to give occupation to his at points of our selection." He further argues that "our concentration at any point compels that of the enemy." It is important that this letter was concerned with Confederate military forces on a wide range of fronts, including Virginia,

North Carolina, and Kentucky. Since it contemplates drawing Federal armies to Confederate points of concentration to "give occupation" to the Federals, the letter is a prescription for military confrontation. It is therefore a statement of an offensive grand strategy, whether the confrontation at the "point of concentration" was to take the form of the tactical offensive or defensive on the part of the South. The second letter to Davis is dated July 6, 1864, shortly after the siege of Petersburg began. Lee wrote: "If we can defeat or drive the armies of the enemy from the field, we shall have peace. All our efforts and energies should be devoted to that object."[5]

This, then, was Lee's view of the way, as Clausewitz defined grand strategy, for the Confederacy "to attain the objects of [the] war." The South was to pursue the military defeat of the North. Lee's offensive grand strategic sense is reiterated again and again in his dispatches to Davis, the War Department, and his fellow general officers. These dispatches, in the *Official Records* and *The Wartime Papers of R. E. Lee*, bristle with offensive rhetoric and planning: "striking a blow," "driving the enemy," "crushing the enemy."[6]

Any doubt that Lee was committed to the offensive as the South's appropriate grand strategy is presumably eliminated when one considers the most obvious source for identifying his grand strategic thinking, the campaigns and battles of the Army of Northern Virginia. Consistent with the grand strategy that he said he believed in and repeatedly planned and advocated, Lee from the beginning embraced the offensive. Appointed to command the Army of Northern Virginia on June 1, 1862, he turned at once to the offensive, beginning with major engagements on the Peninsula—Mechanicsville, Gaines's Mill, Frayser's Farm, and Malvern Hill. Following on the heels of the Seven Days, the Second Bull Run campaign was strategically offensive in an operational sense although, except for Longstreet's counterattack on August 30, it may be classified as defensive from a tactical standpoint. At Antietam Lee stood on the defensive, but the Maryland campaign was strategically offensive; his moving into Maryland assured a major battle in that state. At Chancellorsville, he chose not to retreat when confronted by the Federal pincer movement. Instead, he repeatedly attacked, and the Federals retreated back across the river.

The point is not that each of these campaigns and battles represented an error by Lee. Driving the Federals away from Richmond in 1862, for example, may have been required to maintain Southern morale and to avoid the practical consequences of losing the capital. The point is that the offensive pattern is plain. Lee believed that the South's grand strategic role was offensive.

Lee's grand strategy of the offensive, to defeat the North militarily as distinguished from prolonging the contest until the North gave it up, created a profound problem. It was not feasible and, indeed, was counterproductive to the Confederacy's "objects of war." Curiously, that Lee's attack grand strategy was misplaced is suggested by his own awareness of factors that argued against it. The primary reason the attack grand strategy was counterproductive was numbers, and Lee was sensitive to the South's manpower disadvantage and its implications. A letter of January 10, 1863, to Secretary of War James A. Seddon, between his victory at Fredericksburg and Ambrose E. Burnside's abortive Mud March, reflects this awareness. "I have the honor to represent to you the absolute necessity that exists . . . to increase our armies, if we desire to oppose effectual resistance to the vast numbers that the enemy is now precipitating upon us," Lee wrote. "The great increase of the enemy's forces will augment the disparity of numbers to such a degree that victory, if attained, can only be achieved by a terrible expenditure of the most precious blood of the country."[7]

Further recognition of the numbers problem appears in Lee's letter of June 10, 1863, to Davis, after Chancellorsville and at the outset of the Gettysburg campaign:

> While making the most we can of the means of resistance we possess . . . it is nevertheless the part of wisdom to carefully measure and husband our strength, and not to expect from it more than in the ordinary course of affairs it is capable of accomplishing. We should not therefore conceal from ourselves

that our resources in men are constantly diminishing, and the disproportion in this respect between us and our enemies, if they continue united in their effort to subjugate us, is steadily augmenting. The decrease of the aggregate of this army as disclosed by the returns affords an illustration of this fact. Its effective strength varies from time to time, *but the falling off in its aggregate shows that its ranks are growing weaker and that its losses are not supplied by recruits.* (Emphasis added)[8]

The *Official Records* are full of Lee's analyses of his strength problems. These communications predict that unless his army was reinforced, "the consequences may be disastrous" and include such statements as "I cannot see how we are to escape the natural military consequences of the enemy's numerical superiority."[9]

Consciousness of his numerical disadvantage, of the ever-increasing Federal disproportion, did not mute Lee's commitment to the grand strategic offensive. Nor did that grand strategy permit his army to "husband our strength." During the Seven Days' battles on the Peninsula, George B. McClellan lost approximately 9,796 killed and wounded, 10.7 percent; Lee's casualties were 19,739 men, 20.7 percent of his army. Although Federal casualties in killed and wounded at Second Bull Run exceeded Lee's by approximately 1,000 men, the Army of Northern Virginia lost in excess of 9,000, almost 19 percent as compared to 13.3 percent for the Federals. In spite of McClellan's ineptitude, Lee lost almost 12,000 men, 22.6 percent, at Antietam, immediately following losses in excess of 1,800 at South Mountain on September 14. McClellan's Antietam casualties were 15.5 percent. At Chancellorsville, Lee lost almost 11,000 of 57,000 effectives, in excess of 18 percent, a much higher proportion than Joseph Hooker's 11.4 percent.[10]

These statistics show the serious attrition of Lee's limited numbers. In addition, Lee's losses were mostly irreplaceable, as he was aware. Finally, his losses also seriously affected his army's leadership. "The Confederates' ability to operate as they moved northward was affected by the loss of much mid-level command," Robert K. Krick has written. "The heart of the Confederate Army was starting to feel this difficulty for the first time just *before* Gettysburg. To the tremendous losses of the successful but costly campaign in the summer of 1862 . . . were added the victims of the dreadful bloodshed at Chancellorsville" (emphasis added).[11] Clearly, the Federals' increasingly disproportionate strength was the result of Northern reinforcements, but it was also exacerbated by Lee's heavy, disproportionate, and irreplaceable losses. Had Lee taken the defensive, the increasing Federal manpower advantage would have been slowed.

It is appropriate to contrast the alternative grand strategy of the defensive. In 1986, historians Richard E. Beringer, Herman Hattaway, Archer Jones, and William N. Still, Jr., noted that "no Confederate army lost a major engagement because of the lack of arms, munitions, or other essential supplies." These authors then summarized the case as follows:

> By remarkable and effective efforts the agrarian South did exploit and create an industrial base that proved adequate, with the aid of imports, to maintain suitably equipped forces in the field. Since the Confederate armies suffered no crippling deficiencies in weapons or supply, their principal handicap would be their numerical inferiority. But to offset this lack, Confederates, fighting the first major war in which both sides armed themselves with rifles, had the advantage of a temporary but very significant surge in the power of the tactical defensive. In addition, the difficulties of supply in a very large and relatively thinly settled region proved a powerful aid to strengthening the strategic defensive. Other things being equal, if Confederate military leadership were competent and the Union did not display Napoleonic genius, the tactical and strategic power of the defense could offset northern numerical superiority and presumably give the Confederacy a measure of military victory adequate to maintain its independence.[12]

British observers sensed the feasibility of the grand strategy of the defensive as the war began. Harking back to their own experience in America, they did not see how the South could be conquered. The War of Independence analogy is not perfect, but it is illustrative. The military historian Colonel George A.

Bruce has pointed out that George Washington "had a correct insight into the minds of his own people and that of the enemy, the strength of resolution of each to endure heavy burdens, looking forward with certainty to the time when the public sentiment of England, led by Chatham and Burke, would be ready to acknowledge the Colonies as an independent nation. With these views he carried on the war for seven years, all the way from Boston to Yorktown, on a generally defensive plan, the only one pointing to the final goal of independence"[13] (emphasis added). The Americans, on the grand strategic defensive, lost many battles and retreated many times, but they kept forces in the field to avoid being ultimately defeated, and they won because the British decided that the struggle was either hopeless or too burdensome to pursue.

A Confederate defensive grand strategy would have been premised on E. Porter Alexander's conservative principle "to wear her [the North] out," to "exact . . . such a price in blood & treasure as to exhaust the enthusiasm of its population." To contribute to this wearing out, it was essential for Lee to maintain the viability of his army, to keep it in the field as a genuine force. That viability depended on his retaining sufficient relative strength for mobility and maneuver so as to avoid a siege and also to undertake timely and promising operationally strategic offensives and the tactical offensive. Lee could have accomplished these things had he pursued a defensive grand strategy. And despite Southern manpower disadvantages, this grand strategy was at the outset feasible because of the North's logistical task and the relative power that the rifled gun afforded the defense.

It is to be emphasized that the grand strategy of defense would not have required Southern armies always to be on the strategic operational or tactical defensive. As the British military historian Major General J. F. C. Fuller points out, "It is possible to develop an offensive tactics from a defensive strategy."[14] Thus, if Lee's grand strategic sense of the war had been defensive, he could nevertheless on appropriate occasions have pursued offensive campaigns and offensive tactics in the context of that defensive grand strategy. The Revolution again provides an illustration. Although pursuing a grand strategy of defense, the Americans were sometimes aggressive and offensive, for example, at Trenton, Saratoga, and Yorktown.

The Federal manpower superiority would also have been less significant had Lee assumed the defensive in 1862–63, as evidenced by what happened in the overland campaign in 1864–65. Despite his prior losses and the great Northern numerical superiority, Lee's defense in 1864, again in Alexander's words, exacted "a price in blood" that significantly affected "the enthusiasm of [the North's] population" for continuing the war.[15] Indeed, Lee demonstrated in 1864 the feasibility of the grand strategy of the defense. Had he adopted the defensive earlier he would have had available a reasonable portion of the more than one hundred thousand officers and men that he lost in the offensives in 1862 and 1863, including Gettysburg. With these larger numbers he could have maintained mobility and avoided a siege.

It is in the context of grand strategy that one must view the primary issue regarding Gettysburg, that is, whether Lee should have been there at all. The Gettysburg campaign, Lee's most audacious act, is the apogee of his grand strategy of the offensive. The numerous reasons for the campaign offered by Lee and the commentators are well known: the necessity to upset Federal offensive plans, avoidance of a siege of the Richmond defenses, alleviation of supply problems in unforaged country, encouragement of the peace movement in the North, drawing the Federal army north of the Potomac in order to maneuver, even the relief of Vicksburg. Some or all of these reasons may have contributed to the decision, but fighting a battle was plainly inherent in the campaign because of the foreseeable Federal reaction and because of Lee's intent regarding a battle.

In his outline report dated July 31, 1863, Lee stated that "It had not been intended to fight a general battle at such a distance from our base, unless attacked by the enemy." The foreseeable Federal reaction to Lee's presence in loyal states suggests that the "unless attacked" provision was meaningless. As Hattaway and Jones point out: "Lee could have been under no illusion that he could bring off such a protracted campaign without a battle. ... If he raided enemy territory, it would be politically if not strategically imperative for the Union army to take the offensive."[16] And on June 8, 1863, in a letter to Secretary of War Seddon, he spoke of the "difficulty & hazard in taking the aggressive with so large an army in its front, entrenched behind a river where it cannot be advantageously attacked" and of drawing the enemy out into "a position to be assailed." In the outline report, the same report in which he stated that "it had not been intended to fight a general battle a such a distance from our base," he wrote of his intent to "transfer the scene of hostilities north of the Potomac": "It was thought that the corresponding movements on the part of the enemy to which those contemplated by us would probably give rise, might offer a fair opportunity to *strike a blow* at the army then commanded by General Hooker, and that in any event that army would be compelled to leave Virginia" (emphasis added).[17]

The point is that the Gettysburg campaign involved substantial and unacceptable risks for Lee's army. His northernmost base in Virginia was to be Winchester, after it was taken by Richard S. Ewell. Winchester was ninety miles from Staunton, the available rail terminus. For this reason, and simply because of the distances involved, the extended lines of communication, and the necessity to recross the Potomac, these risks extended to the loss of the Army of Northern Virginia. In any event, assuming victory, the Gettysburg campaign was bound to result in heavy Confederate casualties, as Lee surely knew because of his losses in previous victories and at Antietam. Such foreseeable losses at Gettysburg were bound to limit his army's capacity to maneuver, to contribute to the risk that his army would be fixed, and to increase the risk of his being driven into a siege in the Richmond defenses. Lee had repeatedly said that a siege would be fatal to his army.[18]

Colonel Charles Marshall, whose writings orignated many of the still-current rationalizations of Lee's generalship, set forth what he called "Lee's Military Policy." Having identified the critical importance of the defense of Richmond, Marshall wrote that Lee sought "to employ the enemy at a distance and prevent his near approach to the city." The Maryland campaign and Gettysburg fit this purpose, according to Marshall. But having identified the Confederacy's inherent strength problem, Marshall states that Lee was "unwilling to incur the risks and losses of an aggressive war having for its object the destruction of the enemy." Indeed, wrote Marshall: "General Lee thought that to expose our armies to the sacrifices of great battles the object of which was only to disperse or destroy those of the enemy would soon bring the Confederacy to the verge of exhaustion. Even victory in such engagements might prove disastrous. The North could readily raise new armies, while the means of the South were so limited that a few bloody victories might leave it powerless to continue the struggle."[19]

These are fine words, a prescription for a defensive strategy, but surely they do not describe Lee's military policy. For an accurate description of Lee's leadership one may again consult Major General Fuller, who in 1929 characterized Lee's strategy: "He rushed forth to find a battlefield, to challenge a contest between himself and the North."[20] This is why Lee went north in 1863. It was a continuation of his offensive grand strategy, to "defeat or drive the armies of the enemy from the field." Win, lose, or draw, the Gettysburg campaign was a strategic mistake because of the inevitable casualties that the Army of Northern Virginia could not afford.

In regard to defective execution, it is plain that if an army commander is to undertake a high-risk, strategically offensive maneuver, he had better do it with great care, especially if he is moving into enemy territory with extended lines of communication and endemic relative manpower problems. The fact is that Lee proceeded at Gettysburg without essential control of his army in three crucial respects—reconnaissance, the onset of the battle, and the renewal of the battle on the afternoon of July 1.

In his detailed report of January 1864, Lee made the following statements relating to the reconnaissance: "It was expected that as soon as the Federal Army should cross the Potomac, General Stuart would give notice of its movements, and nothing having been heard from him since our entrance into Maryland, it was inferred that the enemy had not yet left Virginia." This report also recounts Lee's learning from a scout on the night of June 28 that the Army of the Potomac had crossed the river and was approaching South Mountain. Colonel Marshall, who drafted the relevant orders as well as Lee's reports, also states that Lee "had not heard from him [Stuart] since the army left Virginia, and was confident from that fact, in view of the positive orders that Stuart had received, that General Hooker had not yet crossed the Potomac."[21] The facts challenge both the candor of Lee's report and the assumption that Stuart's silence meant that the Army of the Potomac was not following Lee.

In the first place, Lee should have assumed that the Federal army would place itself between him and Washington, by that time a well-developed pattern in the Virginia theater. In addition, dictating the movements of the Army of the Potomac was one of the premises of Lee's movement north. In his outline report of July 31, 1863, Lee stated as an objective of the campaign "the transfer of the scene of hostilities north of the Potomac." He intended, he wrote, that his movement north would provoke "corresponding movements on the part of the enemy . . . and that in any event that army would be compelled to leave Virginia." Lee reiterated the substance of these expectations in his detailed report of January 1864.[22] And as he proceeded, Lee knew considerably more than he admitted in his January 1864 report.

On June 18, Lee advised Davis that "the enemy has been thrown back from the line of the Rappahannock, and is concentrating, as far as I can learn, in the vicinity of Centreville. The last reports from the scouts indicate that he is moving over toward the Upper Potomac." Centreville is about halfway to the Potomac from Fredericksburg. Thus Lee was aware that the Federals were on the move. On June 19, in another communication to Davis, Lee reported that "indications seem to be that his [the enemy's] main body is proceeding toward the

Potomac, whether upon Harper's Ferry or to cross the river east of it, is not yet known." On the following day from Berryville, Virginia, having reported the location of the parts of his own army—Ewell was by this time across the river—Lee again reported what he knew of the Federals: "The movement of the main body . . . is still toward the Potomac, but its real destination is not yet discovered." Three days later, on June 23, another dispatch went to Davis: "Reports of movements of the enemy east of the Blue Ridge cause me to believe that he is preparing to cross the Potomac. A pontoon bridge is said to be laid at Edward's Ferry, and his army corps that he has advanced to Leesburg and the foot of the mountains, appear to be withdrawing." This letter also reported that Ewell was "in motion toward the Susquehanna" and that A. P. Hill's and James Longstreet's corps were nearing the Potomac.[23]

Two more dispatches bear on Lee's expectations. On June 22, in the first of his controversial dispatches to Stuart, he stated that "I fear he [the enemy] will steal a march on us, and get across the Potomac before we are aware." And on June 25, he advised Davis from opposite Williamsport, "I think I can throw General Hooker's Army across the Potomac."[24] From these statements it is apparent that Lee knew that his plan was working—the enemy was following him across the Potomac and out of Virginia. He would have the opportunity to "strike a blow."

On June 22 the much-debated issue of Stuart's orders arose. Lee's cavalry force included, in addition to horse artillery, six brigades under Stuart: Wade Hampton's, Beverly H. Robertson's, William E. "Grumble" Jones's, Fitzhugh Lee's, A. G. Jenkins's, and W. H. F. Lee's, the last-named temporarily commanded by Colonel John R. Chambliss, Jr. Jenkins moved with Ewell, screening the front of the advance, while Robertson and Jones were to guard the mountain passes behind the army. Hampton, Fitz Lee, and Chambliss were to ride with Stuart. Also with the Army of Northern Virginia was Brigadier General John D. Imboden's command of four regiments.[25]

Setting aside postwar recollections of conversations and concentrating on the contemporaneous written word, Lee's

The Advance of Lee's Army Invading the Northern States.
(Frank Leslie's *The Soldier in Our Civil War*)

June 22 communication to Stuart is the first relevant document. This letter, written at Berryville, begins with a direct inquiry regarding the enemy: "Do you know where he is and what he is doing?" The letter then identifies specific assignments for the cavalry brigades with Stuart: "If you find that he [the enemy] is moving northward, and that two brigades can guard the Blue Ridge and take care of your rear, you can move with the other three into Maryland, and take position on General Ewell's right, place yourself in communication with him, guard his flank, keep him informed of the enemy's movements, and collect all the supplies you can for the use of the army."[26]

Lee's June 22 letter to Stuart was sent to General Longstreet for forwarding to Stuart. Lee's letter to Longstreet that accompanied it is lost, but Longstreet's letter of transmittal to Stuart, dated 7:00 P.M. on June 22, refers to Lee's writing of Stuart's "passing by the rear of the enemy" and included advice from Longstreet: "If you can get through by that route, I think that you will be less likely to indicate what our plans are than if you should cross by passing to our rear."[27]

On the following day, June 23, another directive went from Lee to Stuart. Written at 5:00 P.M., it contained the following relevant provisions:

> If General Hooker's army remains inactive, you can leave two brigades to watch him, and withdraw with the three others, but should he not[28] appear to be moving northward I think you had better withdraw this side of the mountain tomorrow night, cross at Shepherdstown the next day, and move to Fredericktown.
>
> You will, however, be able to judge whether you can pass around their army without hindrance, doing them all the damage you can, and cross the river east of the mountains.
>
> In either case, after crossing the river, you must move on and feel the right of Ewell's troops, collecting information, provisions, etc.[29]

This order, like that of June 22, included the instruction to the cavalryman to feel Ewell's right and give Lee information.

Since Lee knew his plan was working and the Federals were following him and were to cross the Potomac, information should have been his concern. In the circumstances, any commander in control of his army would have issued instructions to Stuart that were short, single-minded, and not discretionary. In the June 22 communication, Lee had asked a question regarding the enemy: "Do you know where he is and what he is doing?" He should have told Stuart that this question needed a prompt answer and that Stuart's one task was to keep him constantly informed of the enemy's movements. Lee did not do this, and taken together the orders contain the following problems:

1. No time sequences were specified; no deadlines were stated by which time Stuart was to perform his tasks or make reports.

2. Four missions for the brigades with Stuart were identified in the two orders—guarding Ewell's flank, keeping Ewell informed of the enemy's movements, collecting supplies for the army, and inflicting all possible damage on the Federals.

3. Stuart was to "judge whether you can pass around their army without hindrance." Even Colonel Marshall acknowledges that it was left to "Stuart to decide whether he can move around the Federal army."

4. The reference to Stuart's then "cross[ing] the river east of the mountains" is not specific as to location. Sir Frederick Maurice says that "Lee certainly meant that Stuart was to cross *immediately* east of the mountains, so as to be close to the right flank of the army," but that is not what the communication says.[30]

What fair and reasonable conclusions may be drawn in view of these problems with the orders? In the first place, the orders were ambiguous and uncertain with regard to such critical matters as the times and places of Stuart's movements. Second, contrary to the assertion of some writers, in riding around the Federal army Stuart was manifestly not acting on his own. That ride was expressly contemplated by Lee and was expressly left to Stuart's judgment. Third, regardless of other problems of interpretation, Stuart could not perform reconnaissance

Major General James Ewell Brown Stuart.
(Miller's *Photographic History of the Civil War*)

adequately with so many other tasks to perform. Two of these tasks indeed contradicted the reconnaissance function and minimized the likelihood of success in the performance of that function. Collecting provisions and doing damage to the enemy were sure to draw the cavalry away from the intelligence task and delay its progress, which they did. These collateral missions diminished the intelligence function and diluted the significance of that function. Their existence was bound to have contributed to Stuart's judgment that the ride around the Federals was a reasonable thing to do. Fourth, pushing east around the Union army was inconsistent with protecting the Confederate army's right. Stuart could not effectively protect Ewell's right and at the same time place eighty-five thousand Federals between himself and Ewell.

A fifth conclusion may be drawn regarding the orders to Stuart. Those orders are usually considered in the context of Lee's need for information concerning the movements of the Federal army. They are not analyzed in reference to the movements of the Confederate army after the orders were issued to Stuart. Such an analysis is appropriate.

Lee's entire army was on the move in June 1863. The army commander moves an army and knows where all of its parts are or are supposed to be. The individual parts do not necessarily know where the rest of the army is. A commander in control of his army may not rationally leave the movement of a detached unit up to that unit's commander, in this case Stuart, and then proceed to move the rest of the army and hope that the detached unit will be able to find its way to the moved or moving main body. The army commander is responsible for keeping the detached unit informed. Lee made no plan or timely effort to do this. In his June 22 communication to Stuart, Lee told the cavalry leader that the army's advance, Ewell's corps, was to move toward the Susquehanna River via Emmitsburg and Chambersburg. The June 23 order stated that "the movements of Ewell's corps are as stated in my former letter. Hill's first division will reach the Potomac to-day, and Longstreet will follow tomorrow."

These messages were the last Stuart received from Lee before the cavalry moved out on the night of June 24 to begin the fateful ride around the Federals. Thus there was justice to Stuart's complaint in his defensive official report that when he started east he understood that the rest of the army was moving toward the Susquehanna. Accordingly, he stated that when he swung north he moved toward York to rendezvous, only to discover that the Confederates had left that area. His sole source of information regarding the Confederate army's location was Northern newspapers. Finally, on the night of July 1, he received a dispatch from Lee telling him that the army was at Gettysburg.

There is a final conclusion that may be drawn regarding reconnaissance. Stuart had been given the discretion to "pass around their army," with no time or distance limitations. Having in mind that Lee knew the Federal army was following him, a reconnaissance contingency plan was surely in order. There was also justification for Stuart's statement in his report that if cavalry "in advance of the army the first day of Gettysburg" was wanted, "it must be remembered that the cavalry [Jenkins's brigade] specially selected for advance guard to the army by the commanding general on account of its geographical location at the time, was available for this purpose." Kenneth P. Williams's observation is fair: "There were still three cavalry brigades near at hand that he [Lee] could have called upon for mounted service: Imboden's operating toward the west, and those of B. H. Robertson and W. E. Jones guarding the passes below the Potomac that soon needed little or no guarding. There seems to be no excuse for Lee's finding himself at Chambersburg on the 28th without a single regiment of cavalry."[31]

This, then, was the Confederate reconnaissance failure as the armies moved toward July 1, 1863, and this failure was essentially Lee's.

The second leadership error in execution on July 1 concerns the onset of the battle. Coddington states that "to say that Stuart's late arrival was a major cause of Lee's defeat is a little too pat an answer to the question of why the Confederates lost the battle." There were other command failures. Colonel

Marshall speaks of the Gettysburg campaign as involving the "risk [of] the battlefield which chance might bring us during a movement northward."[32] As it turned out, it was simply a chance battlefield.

In his July 31, 1863, outline report, part of which has been previously quoted, Lee states: "It had not been intended to fight a general battle at such a distance from our base, unless attacked by the enemy, but, finding ourselves unexpectedly confronted by the Federal Army, it became a matter of difficulty to withdraw through the mountains with our large trains. At the same time, the country was unfavorable for collecting supplies while in the presence of the enemy's main body. . . . A battle thus became in a measure unavoidable."[33]

In their essentials, these words bear little resemblance to what Lee in fact intended or what in fact occurred. In the same report, he stated that his movement was intended to require Hooker to move with him and that this "might offer a fair opportunity to strike a blow" at the Federals. With regard to the "unless attacked" condition of the report, Lee was not attacked. His forces initially attacked and were the aggressor for three days. As a result of the initial attack, a battle occurred on July 1, not by plan but by chance.

Had Lee seriously intended to avoid a chance battle, he could have so instructed his corps commanders. The *Official Records* contain no such circular. Lee's reports do not say that he had issued any such order. Nor do the reports of Hill, Ewell, or Longstreet. Even after he learned on the night of June 28 that the Army of the Potomac had, as he expected, crossed the river, there is no evidence of warning orders. No such orders were forthcoming before July 1, and the battle and the battlefield were left to chance until it was too late because he had not asserted control over his army. This was his second failure of control.

Lee provided a laconic account of the start of the battle in his official report dated July 31, 1863. "The leading division of Hill met the enemy in advance of Gettysburg on the morning of July 1," he wrote. "Driving back these troops to within a short distance of the town, he there encountered a larger force, with which two of his divisions became engaged. Ewell, coming up with two of his divisions by Heidlersburg road, joined in the engagement." The battle thus began without Lee's knowing the location of other elements of the Federal army and without the Confederate army's being closed up. On June 30 Henry Heth had sent James J. Pettigrew's brigade from Cashtown to Gettysburg and discovered the enemy, principally cavalry, there. Lee was at Chambersburg. Hill's November 1863 report states: "A courier was then dispatched with this information to the general commanding . . . ; also to General Ewell, informing him, and that I intended to advance the next morning and discover what was in my front." As Coddington notes, Hill's "announcement seemed not to have disturbed the commanding general."[34]

As that fateful July 1 began, conservative instincts came over Lee, and he briefly and belatedly asserted himself to control events. Thus Ewell's 1863 report of the campaign recites that at Heidlersburg on the night of June 30 he received Lee's order to proceed to Cashtown or Gettysburg "as circumstances might dictate," together with a note from Hill saying that he was at Cashtown. On July 1, Ewell reported that he started for Cashtown and Hunterstown. Receiving a note from Hill telling of his advance on Gettysburg, Ewell ordered Robert E. Rodes's and Jubal A. Early's divisions toward that place. Ewell notified Lee of these movements and was informed by Lee that, "in case we found the enemy's forces very large, he did not want a general engagement brought on till the rest of the army came up." Ewell's report continued: "By the time this message reached me, General A. P. Hill had already been warmly engaged with a large body of the enemy in his front, and Carter's artillery battalion, of Rodes' division, had opened with fine effect on the flank of the same body, which was rapidly preparing to attack me, while fresh masses were moving into position in my front. It was too late to avoid an engagement without abandoning the position already taken up, and I determined to push the attack vigorously."[35] In short, Lee's attempt at control came too late because of his failure to react to Hill's June 30 communication and because of the onrush of events.

Lee's renewal of the battle on July 1 constitutes the third error in execution. He apparently did make a second effort at control when he became aware of the fighting at Gettysburg. This awareness, Coddington states, occurred while Lee rode from Chambersburg to Cashtown, where he and his party heard the sound of cannon fire to the east. Walter H. Taylor adds that at Cashtown Lee received a communication from Hill and that he then sent instructions to Heth to avoid a general engagement but to ascertain the enemy's force and report immediately. A. L. Long confirms the Cashtown report from Hill but states that it was a request for reinforcements and that Lee rushed Richard H. Anderson's division forward. General W. N. Pendleton, who was with Lee, mentions the sound of cannon fire. He reports further that the command party hastened toward Gettysburg and that, "arriving near the crest of an eminence more than a mile west of the town . . . we took positions overlooking the field. It was, perhaps, 2 o'clock, and the battle was raging with considerable violence. . . . Observing the course of events, the commanding general suggested whether positions on the right could not be found to enfilade the valley between our position and the town and the enemy's batteries next the town."[36]

Pendleton's account suggests that if Lee, aware of Heth's morning attack, instructed Heth to avoid a general engagement, he abandoned this caution when he reached the field. And Coddington, relying on Heth's postwar account, confirms Lee's decision to commit the Confederates to the afternoon attack. Coddington tells of Heth's observation of Rodes's becoming engaged and states: "[Heth] took the trouble to find Lee and seek his permission to attack in coordination with Rodes. Lee refused the request on the grounds that Longstreet was not up. Returning to his division, Heth saw the enemy shifting his weight to meet Rodes's attack. He again sought Lee's consent to give assistance, and this time received it. These meetings of the two generals occurred before the grand assault all along the Union line."[37]

Thus did Lee permit the renewal of the battle in the afternoon of July 1 in spite of his lack of knowledge of the Federal army's whereabouts and the absence of his own First Corps, which meant that he did it without having reason to believe that he had sufficient manpower to deprive the Federals of the high ground south of the town. Laxness with respect to reconnaissance and his lack of control of Hill's movements had caused him to stumble into a battle. The renewal of the battle represents Lee's third failure with respect to the events of July 1. It committed him to a major confrontation on this particular ground. The need for food and forage did not require his renewal of the battle on July 1 any more than they did on the days following July 1. Porter Alexander, referring to July 2 and the retreat to the Potomac, notes that the Confederates foraged successfully for more than a week in a restricted area of Pennsylvania. He also states that it was feasible for the Confederates to have abandoned Seminary Ridge on the night of July 1 or on July 2: "The onus of attack was upon Meade. . . . We could even have fallen back to Cashtown & held the mountain passes . . . & popular sentiment would have forced Meade to take the aggressive."[38] This was even more true in the early afternoon of July 1, when Lee authorized the all-out Confederate attack on Seminary Ridge, without sufficient troops of his own on hand to keep going and without knowledge of the whereabouts of the rest of the Federal army.

At the close of the day, the net effect of his command failure was that Lee was on the battlefield and in the battle that chance had brought him. As a consequence, he was significantly disadvantaged: he confronted an enemy that occupied what Porter Alexander called a "really wonderful position," with interior lines; Lee's line was a long exterior line, a difficult one from which to organize a coordinated attack; and four of his divisions, as Lee reported, were "weakened and exhausted by a long and bloody struggle."[39]

Committed to the Lee tradition, a number of commentators in the *Southern Historical Society Papers* and elsewhere have attempted to rationalize his command failures in regard to July 1. As has been indicated, Stuart's absence is a major thrust of these efforts. Blaming Hill, in spite of Lee's knowledge on June 30 of Hill's planned movements on July 1, is another. Lee's advocates also attempt to moot the issue of his command failures by placing blame on Ewell. They argue that these failures would have been irrelevant if only Ewell had pushed on late on July 1 and seized Cemetery Hill or Culp's Hill. It is argued that this could have been readily accomplished. A number of Confederate officers said so—after the war and when the Lee tradition of invincibility was being formed.[40] A good lawyer may reasonably be skeptical of the *Southern Historical Society Papers* as evidence. Written after the facts during the creation of the Lost Cause tradition, their value as history is surely limited. Like the patriarchal stories of the Old Testament, such accounts have ideological rather than historical value. They nevertheless require a response.

An initial difficulty in regard to the controversy about Ewell's conduct concerns identification of the issue. The advocates on both sides insist on debating whether or not Ewell would have been successful. This is inevitably a hypothetical question and therefore inappropriate for historical inquiry. Properly framed, the issue historically can only be whether Ewell made a reasonable decision in the circumstances. There is a second problem. Those who criticize Ewell frequently resort to a contention that is also inappropriate: regardless of the facts, Ewell "should have tried." They forget that Ewell was not a Civil War student. He was a general officer responsible for the consequences of his acts and for the lives of his soldiers. Finally, the partisans frequently overlook the fact that there was more involved for the Confederates than simply getting on the heights. There was also the question of whether they would be able to stay if the Federals were to mount a prompt effort to drive them off.

With the foregoing considerations in mind, one may pursue the question of whether Ewell made a rational decision. This is a matter of the evidence with respect to four factors: the nature of the terrain, the Federal forces opposed, the manpower available to Ewell, and the orders given to Ewell by Lee.

The terrain confronting Ewell may be seen today looking up from the area of the Culp House and the low ground immediately to the west of that house. The heights are precipitous, irregular, and complex, marked by hollows and ravines. An attacking force would have been advancing uphill against defenders with ample places from which to effect an ambush.

In considering the Federal forces opposed—and the troops Ewell could have used—the identification of precise times of day is an impossible task. Any discussion of the issue is limited by inability to state exactly when either Federal or Confederate units were available. Nevertheless, Federals to oppose an attack were on the heights or very close by during the general time period in which Ewell was considering the question:

1. One brigade of Adolph von Steinwehr's division and Michael Wiedrich's battery had been on Cemetery Hill since the arrival of the Eleventh Corps.

2. The remnant of the Iron Brigade, approximately seven hundred men, had been sent from Cemetery to Culp's Hill and was entrenching there in a strong position.

3. The 7th Indiana of Lysander Cutler's brigade, five hundred rifles, which had not been engaged, had arrived and had been sent to Culp's Hill with the members of that brigade who had come through the day's fighting.

4. The remaining effectives from the First Corps and Eleventh Corps, "basically intact" according to Harry W. Pfanz, were present. There were skirmishers in the town at the base of Cemetery Hill.

5. The Federals had a total of forty guns and ample ammunition on the heights.

6. Henry W. Slocum's Twelfth Corps was close by, approximately one mile from the scene. John W. Geary's division was on the Federal left by approximately 5:00 P.M.; the first division was on the Federal right at about the same time.[41]

Confederate perceptions of this opposition are illuminating. In his 1863 report, Rodes stated that before "the completion of his defeat before the town, the enemy had begun to establish a line of battle on the heights back of the town, and by the time my line was in a condition to renew the attack, he displayed quite a formidable line of infantry and artillery immediately in my front, extending smartly to my right, and as far as I could see to my left, in front of Early." Ewell's 1863 report was similar: "The enemy had fallen back to a commanding position known as Cemetery Hill . . . and quickly showed a formidable front there. . . . I could not bring artillery to bear on it."[42] There were, in short, substantial forces opposed to Ewell, infantry and artillery, placed on imposing terrain.

With regard to the manpower available for the attack, each of the Confederate corps on hand was missing a division. In the case of Ewell, Edward "Allegheny" Johnson's division was not present. It arrived at a late hour. From Hill's corps, Anderson's division did not come up until after the day closed. Lee's detailed report describes the four divisions that had participated in the July I fight as "already weakened and exhausted by a long and bloody struggle." Hill reported that his two divisions were "exhausted by some six hours hard fighting [and that] prudence led me to be content with what had been gained, and not push forward troops exhausted and necessarily disordered, probably to encounter fresh troops of the enemy." Ewell's report similarly noted that "all the troops with me were jaded by twelve hours' marching and fighting."[43] And the Confederate reports uniformly state that the Southern units had lost formation at the conclusion of the movement that drove the Federals from Seminary Ridge. Ewell's task was not simply to continue an organized assault that was ongoing. He would have been required to marshal forces and undertake a new movement against the heights.

Douglas Southall Freeman, Lee's great advocate, is always anxious to rationalize Lee's failures at the expense of his lieutenants. In *Lee's Lieutenants*, he criticizes Ewell for not mooting Confederate problems on the first day by taking the heights. He describes in detail Ewell's communications at this hour and his efforts to organize the forces with which to attack. Having recounted Lee's advising Ewell that none of Hill's troops were available on Ewell's right, Freeman states: "All of this meant that if Cemetery Hill was to be taken, Ewell must

do it with his own men." Noting then that Early had detached
two brigades under John B. Gordon to operate on Ewell's left,
Freeman says: "Still again, the force with which Ewell could
attack immediately was small. . . . Two Brigades of Early, then,
and the tired survivors of Rodes's confused charges—these
were all Ewell had for the attack till Johnson arrived. Nor
would this force . . . have any support from the right."[44] Even
Freeman concedes that Ewell did not have significant numbers
for the attack.

Finally, what were Ewell's orders? Lee's detailed report identifies them and also their logic:

> It was ascertained . . . that the remainder of that army [the Fed-
> eral army] . . . was approaching Gettysburg. Without informa-
> tion as to its proximity, the strong position which the enemy
> had assumed could not be attacked without danger of exposing
> the four divisions present, already weakened and exhausted by a
> long and bloody struggle, to an overwhelming number of fresh
> troops. General Ewell was, therefore, instructed to carry the hill
> occupied by the enemy, if he found it practicable, but to avoid
> a general engagement until the arrival of the other divisions
> of the army. . . . He decided to await Johnson's division,
> which . . . did not reach Gettysburg until a late hour.[45]

In *Lee's Lieutenants*, Freeman covers this issue in a chapter
titled "Ewell Cannot Reach a Decision."[46] Surely this is non-
sense. Pursuant to Lee's order, Ewell decided that it was not
"practicable" to attack. Lee was on Seminary Ridge and available. The plain fact is that he did not issue a peremptory order
to Ewell for the reasons he states in his report: the Federal
army was approaching, but its proximity was unknown; the
"strong position" of the enemy; the worn condition of the
Confederate forces available; the risk of the presence of overwhelming and fresh Federal troops; and the desire to avoid a
general engagement.

It is unhistoric to conclude that Ewell was necessarily wrong
in his judgment. His decision was reasonable in the circumstances, and that responds to the only historically appropriate
question concerning Ewell's conduct.

One can only conclude that Lee's movement across the Potomac was a grave strategic error. In addition, in reference to the first day of the battle, there were significant command failures on Lee's part that were destructive to the Confederate chances of victory at Gettysburg.

Confederate Corps Leadership on the First Day at Gettysburg

A. P. Hill and Richard S. Ewell in a Difficult Debut

GARY W. GALLAGHER

ormer Confederates pursued the question of responsibility for the defeat at Gettysburg with almost religious zeal in the years following Appomattox. Accusations about the culpability of Lee's principal lieutenants had surfaced well before the end of the war, but not until the mid-1870s did the debate take on the character of an internecine brawl. At the heart of the controversy lay an attempt on the part of Jubal A. Early, Fitzhugh Lee, J. William Jones, and others to refute James Longstreet's suggestion, first given wide circulation in William Swinton's history of the Army of the Potomac, that Lee had erred badly at Gettysburg. Early and the others sought to absolve Lee of responsibility for any military failures during the war and singled out Longstreet as their primary villain. Longstreet had ignored orders to launch an assault against the Federal left at dawn on July 2, they argued, thereby denying the South a victory at Gettysburg and probably its independence. Although Longstreet stood at the vortex of this war of words, other ranking Confederates also received substantial criticism during and after the war—"Jeb" Stuart for a ride around the Union army that prevented his keeping Lee informed of Federal movements, A. P. Hill for precipitating the battle against Lee's orders and then mounting a weak pursuit of routed Federals, and Richard Stoddert Ewell for failing to seize Cemetery Hill and Culp's Hill late in the first day's fighting.[1]

Lost opportunities on July 1 loomed large because the troops of Hill and Ewell had gained a decided advantage over their opponents north and west of Gettysburg by midafternoon. To many Southern observers it seemed that one more round of assaults would have carried Cemetery Hill and Culp's Hill and sealed a major victory. Loath to engage the enemy in the first place, Lee had reached the field in time to recognize the opening presented by Hill's earlier decision to commit two divisions and had sought to press the Confederate advantage. But first Hill and then Ewell declined to renew the offensive, observed their critics, affording the desperate Federals time to patch together a strong line on high ground below the town. Their failure set the stage for two more days of bloody battle during which the commanders of the Second and Third corps became little more than bystanders in a drama dominated on the Confederate side by Lee and Longstreet.

Hill and Ewell entered Pennsylvania in June 1863 burdened with the legacy of "Stonewall" Jackson. Between them they commanded the four divisions of the old Second Corps. Lee's reorganization of the army after Jackson's death had assigned three of Jackson's divisions to Ewell as chief of a smaller Second Corps, while Hill's Light Division, long a bulwark of Jackson's corps, supplied six of the thirteen brigades in "Little Powell's" new Third Corps.[2] Perhaps inevitably, estimates of the performances of Hill and Ewell on July 1 frequently included invidious comparisons to Jackson—always to the "Mighty Stonewall" of the Valley and Chancellorsville rather than to the eminently fallible "Old Jack" of the Seven Days or Cedar Mountain.

Less than a month after Gettysburg, Surgeon Spencer Glasgow Welch of the 13th South Carolina complained to his wife that Hill had mishandled his troops on July 1. Had he not done so, the Third Corps could have captured "the strong position last occupied by the enemy . . . and the next day when Ewell and Longstreet came up the victory completely won." "If 'Old Stonewall' had been alive and there," suggested Welch (whose regiment remained in the Second Corps), "it no doubt would have been done. Hill was a good division commander, but he is not a superior corps commander. He lacks the mind and sagacity of Jackson." Henry Heth's division led the Third Corps toward Gettysburg and suffered severe casualties during the fighting on July 1. Writing about the battle in 1877, Heth refrained from making direct comments about Hill's actions but did mention the public's questioning "whether if Stonewall Jackson had been in command of Hill's corps on the first day— July 1st—a different result would have been obtained."[3]

Other critics focused on Hill's decision to send Heth's division into Gettysburg despite Lee's orders to avoid a general engagement. In his history of Virginia during the war, Jedediah Hotchkiss observed that "A. P. Hill, always ready and anxious for a fight, but so far as known without orders from General Lee, sent the divisions of Heth and Pender toward Gettysburg. . . . [He thus] brought on an engagement with two corps of Meade's army." The careful Porter Alexander averred that "Hill's movement to Gettysburg was made of his own motion, and with knowledge that he would find the enemy's cavalry in possession." "Lee's orders were to avoid bringing on an action," continued Alexander, who added that Hill's "venture is another illustration of an important event allowed to happen without supervision." No postwar critic savaged Hill more completely than John S. Mosby. In an extended apology for Jeb Stuart's absence from the army, the famous guerrilla insisted that Hill miscalculated in sending Heth's division toward Gettysburg on the morning of July 1. "Hill and Heth in their reports, to save themselves from censure, call the first day's action a reconnaissance; this is all an afterthought," wrote Mosby. "They wanted to conceal their responsibility for the final defeat. Hill said he felt the need of cavalry—then he ought to have stayed in camp and waited for the cavalry." No one ordered Hill to advance, concluded Mosby, and Lee "never would have sanctioned it."[4]

Modern historians have joined this chorus. For example, in his massive chronicle of the artillery in Lee's army, Jennings C. Wise observed that Hill's "orders were specific not to bring on an action, but his thirst for battle was unquenchable, and . . . he rushed on, and . . . took the control of the situation out of the hands of the commander-in-chief." Warren W. Hassler's *Crisis at the Crossroads*, the only general monograph

Lieutenant General Ambrose Powell Hill.
(Miller's *Photographic History of the Civil War*)

devoted to the action on July 1, stated unequivocally that "Hill certainly erred, as evidenced by Lee's later painful surprise, in permitting Heth to march on Gettysburg for forage and shoes." Hassler believed that Hill should have exercised greater caution "in developing the situation in the event that Federal troops were present there in numbers." Even Edwin B. Coddington, whose admirable study of the campaign set a standard for meticulous scholarship, speculated that Hill expected to find a fight as well as some shoes and provisions on the morning of July 1. Mosby may have been correct, stated Coddington, "when he charged Hill with planning a 'foray' and calling it a 'reconnaissance.'" Douglas Southall Freeman labeled the manner in which the Army of Northern Virginia stumbled into a confrontation on the first day "incautious," apportioning most of the responsibility to Jeb Stuart. "Obvious blame, also, would be charged against Powell Hill," remarked Freeman, "if he had not been sick on the 1st." That illness prevented his monitoring Heth's advance more closely and, in Freeman's view, absolved him of criticism.[5]

Richard S. Ewell's decision not to attack Cemetery Hill and Culp's Hill on the afternoon of July 1 inspired more heated discussion—and more direct comparisons with Jackson—than did Hill's conduct. Major General Isaac Ridgeway Trimble held no command on July 1 but found himself in Gettysburg with Ewell about midafternoon. "The fighting ceased about 3 P.M.," Trimble noted in his diary, "Genl. Ewell saying he did not wish to bring on a hurried engagement without orders from Lee. This was *a radical error,* for had we continued the fight, we should have got in their rear & taken the Cemetery Hill & Culps Hill." Trimble expanded on his diary entry in a speech prepared after the war and published in the 1870s. He described a tense confrontation between himself and Ewell, during which he told Ewell that Culp's Hill held the key to the Federal position and advised that a brigade be sent to occupy it. Ewell asked if Trimble were certain the hill commanded the town, prompting Trimble to reply that the general could see for himself that it did and ought to be seized at once. "General

Ewell made some impatient reply," remembered Trimble, "and the conversation dropped."[6]

Junior officers also sensed a passing opportunity. J. A. Stikeleather of the 4th North Carolina, a regiment in S. Dodson Ramseur's brigade of Robert E. Rodes's division, entered Gettysburg on the heels of the retreating Federals and estimated that five hundred troops could have captured Cemetery Hill at that point. "The simplest soldier in the ranks felt it," he wrote his mother soon after the battle. "But, timidity in the commander that stepped into the shoes of the fearless Jackson, prompted delay, and all night long the busy axes from tens of thousands of busy hands on that crest, rang out clearly on the night air, and bespoke the preparation the enemy were making for the morrow." Another Confederate witness, writing twenty-two years after the battle, professed to have heard Brigadier General Harry Hays urge Jubal Early to strike Culp's Hill with his entire division. Early agreed that the eminence "should be occupied on the spot" but felt constrained by Ewell's orders not to advance beyond the town. Turning away from Hays and the writer, Early then muttered, "more to himself than Hays, 'If Jackson were on the field I would act on the spot.' "[7]

Influential postwar accounts by Henry Kyd Douglas and John B. Gordon were equally damning. Douglas recalled in his memoirs written shortly after the war (but not published until 1940) that Ewell's staff lost heart when the general failed to follow his initial success with an assault against Cemetery Hill. According to Douglas, chief of staff Sandie Pendleton, when just out of Ewell's hearing, said "quietly and with much feeling, 'Oh, for the presence and inspiration of Old Jack for just one hour!' " Gordon characteristically placed himself at center stage in a dramatic account. His brigade, which belonged to Early's division, had pursued the broken Federals into Gettysburg; looking southward toward the high ground, Gordon saw an opening and believed that in "less than half an hour my troops would have swept up and over those hills, the possession of which was of such momentous consequence." Two times, claimed Gordon, he ignored instructions to halt: "Not until the third or fourth order of the most peremptory character reached me did I obey." "No soldier in a great crisis ever wished more ardently for a deliverer's hand," stated Gordon, "than I wished for one hour of Jackson when I was ordered to halt. Had he been there, his quick eye would have caught at a glance the entire situation, and instead of halting me he would have urged me forward and have pressed the advantage to the utmost."[8]

Though he gave no hint of it in his official report or correspondence with President Davis, R. E. Lee apparently also felt keen disappointment in Ewell. He told former Second Corps chief of ordnance William Allan in April 1868 that he could not get Ewell "to act with decision." "Stuart's failure to carry out his instructions *forced the battle of Gettysburg*," Allan paraphrased Lee in notes written immediately after their conversation, "& *the imperfect, halting way in which his corps commanders* (especially Ewell) *fought the battle, gave victory . . . finally to the foe.*" Nearly two years later, Lee confided to Allan that he often thought that "if Jackson had been there [at Gettysburg] he would have succeeded."[9] Three months before he died Lee discussed Gettysburg with his cousin Cassius Lee, again saying that Jackson's presence would have brought victory. "Ewell was a fine officer," Lee commented, "but would never take the responsibility of exceeding his orders, and having been ordered to Gettysburg, he would not go farther and hold the heights beyond the town."[10]

In the face of such an array of evidence (and these examples only hint at its extent), it is scarcely surprising that most historians have taken Ewell to task for his decision not to assault Cemetery Hill. Douglas Southall Freeman's handling of this phase of Gettysburg in *Lee's Lieutenants* appears in a chapter titled "Ewell Cannot Reach a Decision." Granting Ewell every extenuating circumstance, concluded Freeman, the "impression persists that he did not display the initiative, resolution and boldness to be expected of a good soldier." Clifford Dowdey, whose gracefully written books on Lee and his army gained wide popularity, portrayed Ewell as a man frozen by irresolution, dependent upon Jubal Early's counsel, and fearful of Lee's adverse opinion. By the evening of July 1, argued Dowdey, Lee realized that "paralysis of will marked Ewell like a fatal disease. . . . [He] saw that Jackson's great subordinate had failed in his hour of decision." Hill had drawn Lee into a battle he did not want, believed Dowdey; then "the commander of the mobile Second Corps had robbed the army of its chance to win the field." Warren Hassler hedged on the issue of Cemetery Hill and Culp's Hill: "Ewell—a new corps commander—proved that he was by no means up to stepping into Jackson's shoes and filling them, though he was perhaps correct in not launching an attack on these eminences, as the Unionists, by 5 o'clock, were well on their way toward rendering the elevations impregnable." Coddington defended Ewell's decision not to order an assault more directly, though he, too, could not resist adding that if "Ewell had been a Jackson he might have been able to regroup his forces quickly enough to attack within an hour after the Yankees had started to retreat through the town."[11]

Any judgments about the conduct of Hill and Ewell on July 1 necessarily rest on an imperfect body of evidence. It is important to evaluate the individuals who kept diaries, wrote letters or memoirs, or reported on conversations they overheard. Did they have motivations that colored their accounts? For example, it is possible that Trimble, a major general without portfolio, resented Ewell's offhand dismissal of his counsel and consequently exaggerated the lieutenant general's confusion. It is also pertinent to inquire whether soldiers who had fought under Jackson in the glory days of the Second Corps too quickly assumed that their old chief might have acted differently and accomplished more. Finally, did writers unintentionally (or intentionally) allow postwar interpretations to shape their testimony as eyewitnesses?

Among the leading examples of participants whose postwar writings must be used with great care is John B. Gordon. Few witnesses matched Gordon in his egocentrism or his willingness to play loose with the truth, and his recollections leave unwary readers with a distinct impression that the South

Brigadier General John Brown Gordon.
(Courtesy of the Library of Congress)

would have triumphed if only misguided superiors such as Ewell and Early had acted on his advice. Henry Kyd Douglas displayed similar tendencies to magnify his own role and opt for the embellished anecdote rather than mundane fact—a circumstance that has led some to suggest that his book should be titled "Stonewall Rode with Me" rather than "I Rode with Stonewall." Yet each of these men saw so much and wrote so well that their books are cited with great frequency in the literature. Modern judgments based on such testimony necessarily reflect the flaws of the originals.[12]

It is especially important to employ discrimination in using literature that embraces the myth of the Lost Cause, much of which sought to canonize Lee. As a rough yardstick, students may assume that the later the account by a soldier, the less likely it will be to offer dispassionate analysis of Lee (there are exceptions to this rule, E. Porter Alexander's writings being the most obvious). Jubal Early anticipated this trend in postwar literature with the publication of his address on Lee delivered at Washington and Lee University on the general's birthday in 1872. After cataloging great captains through the ages, Early assured his listeners that "it is a vain work for us to seek anywhere for a parallel to the great character which has won our admiration and love. Our beloved Chief stands, like some lofty column which rears its head among the highest, in grandeur, simple, pure and sublime, needing no borrowed lustre; and he is all our own." This vision of Lee precluded serious criticism lest an author raise doubts about his own Southern loyalty, a fact not lost on those who wrote about the campaigns of the Army of Northern Virginia. This is not to say that the dozens of articles published in the *Southern Historical Society Papers*, in which Early and others orchestrated a massive examination of Gettysburg, and the vast body of other postwar testimony cannot be used with profit. Indeed, some of the most valuable information on the Confederate side of the campaign resides in such sources. But readers should be aware that they contain much special pleading, selective recall, and outright falsehood.[13]

Just as the evidence relating to Hill and Ewell on July 1 must not be accepted uncritically at face value, so also must modern students resist the temptation to judge the generals outside of their historical context. Both men made decisions based on available intelligence about the Union army and an imperfect understanding of the terrain. What they did not know should not be used against them. For example, many writers have buttressed their case against Ewell by quoting a letter written in January 1878 by Winfield Scott Hancock to Fitzhugh Lee. "In my opinion," stated Hancock in response to a query from Lee, "if the Confederates had continued the pursuit of General Howard on the afternoon of the 1st July at Gettysburg, they would have driven him over and beyond Cemetery Hill." Such a statement from the man who commanded the Federal defense late on the first day seemingly carried great weight. But should it? Hancock knew how weak the Federal defenders were at that point in the battle; Ewell did not and should not be criticized for failing to understand the situation on high ground he could not see.[14]

Factors such as the nature of Lee's orders, the condition of Hill's and Ewell's troops following their midafternoon success, problems of communication, and the normal chaos of a large battlefield also should be weighed. Finally, the fair question is whether Hill and Ewell discharged their duties reasonably well on July 1—not whether they matched the standard of excellence set by Stonewall Jackson in the campaigning from Second Manassas through Chancellorsville.

Hill almost certainly went into the Gettysburg campaign with his commanding general's full confidence. As early as October 1862, Lee had told Jefferson Davis that next to Jackson and Longstreet, "I consider A. P. Hill the best commander with me. He fights his troops well, and takes good care of them." "At present," added Lee, "I do not think that more than two commanders of corps are necessary for this army." Eight months later, in the wake of Jackson's death, Lee opted to add a third corps. "I have for the past year felt that the corps of this army were too large for one commander," Lee explained to the president (contradicting his statement of October 1862). "Nothing prevented my proposing to you to reduce their size and increase their number but my inability to recommend commanders." Now he reaffirmed his belief that Hill was "the best soldier of his grade" with the army and asked Davis to agree to his heading the new Third Corps.[15] Hill took his famous Light Division, less two brigades and led by William Dorsey Pender, with him from the Second to the Third Corps; there it joined Richard H. Anderson's division, shifted over from Longstreet's First Corps, and a new division under Henry Heth composed of two brigades from the Light Division and a pair of others transferred to the army from Mississippi and North Carolina.

As the bulk of the Army of Northern Virginia prepared to march toward the Potomac during the first week in June, Lee instructed Hill to watch and react to the Army of the Potomac along the Rappahannock River line. "You are desired to open any official communications sent to me," the commanding general told his lieutenant, "and, if necessary, act upon them, according to the dictates of your good judgment." Reminiscent of the freedom previously accorded Jackson, this grant of wide discretion suggests that Lee harbored few doubts about Hill's ability to restrain the headlong impulse to fight that had been so obvious in his conduct at Mechanicsville and elsewhere.[16]

Hill's first substantial test in his new position came on July 1 and raised questions about his impetuosity as well as his broader capacity to command a corps. Did he needlessly trigger a battle Lee hoped to avoid? And once on the verge of sweeping success late in the afternoon, did he fail to use his men to best advantage? Affirmative answers to these questions not only constitute an indictment of Hill's generalship, but they also affect any assessment of Lee's role in shaping the ultimate Confederate defeat.

Lee learned from Longstreet's scout Harrison on the night of June 28 that the Federal army had crossed the Potomac. In the absence of more substantial intelligence from his own cavalry—and fearing a Union movement against his supply line in the Cumberland Valley—Lee aborted a planned movement toward Harrisburg and issued orders on June 29 for the reconcentration of the Army of Northern Virginia on the east side of the South Mountain range. Hill and Longstreet were "to proceed from Chambersburg to Gettysburg," toward which point Ewell's divisions would march from their positions to the north and east.[17]

A surgeon on James Longstreet's staff remembered a relaxed Lee talking to a group of officers at his headquarters shortly after dispatching these orders: "To-morrow, gentlemen, we will not move to Harrisburg as we expected, but will go over to Gettysburg and see what General Meade is after." Heth's division of Hill's corps led the way eastward from Chambersburg to Cashtown, a hamlet eight miles west of Gettysburg, on the twenty-ninth; Pender and the Light Division followed the next day, and Anderson's orders called for his division to take the same route on July 1.[18]

On the morning of June 30, Heth sent his largest brigade, four North Carolina regiments under James Johnston Pettigrew, to Gettysburg in search of shoes and other supplies. A nonprofessional soldier who had compiled a dazzling record as a student at the University of North Carolina, Pettigrew spotted Northern cavalry as he neared the western edge of Gettysburg and elected to withdraw rather than risk battle against a foe of unknown size and composition. He subsequently told Heth about the Federal cavalry, adding that some of his officers also had heard drums on the far side of Gettysburg, indicating the presence of Union infantry. Hill soon joined Heth and Pettigrew, and the brigadier repeated his story. Hill doubted that Pettigrew had seen more than a small detachment (he had in fact seen part of John Buford's two full brigades): "I am just from General Lee, and the information he has from his scouts corroborates that I have received from mine—that is, the enemy are still at Middleburg [some sixteen miles from Gettysburg], and have not yet struck their tents."[19]

There may have been some of the West Pointer's disdain for civilian soldiers manifest in this discussion—a professional questioning a talented amateur's observations. Perhaps sensing this, Pettigrew asked Captain Louis G. Young of his staff, who knew Hill from their service together during the Seven Days, to speak to the corps commander. Young insisted that the troops he saw were veterans rather than Home Guards;

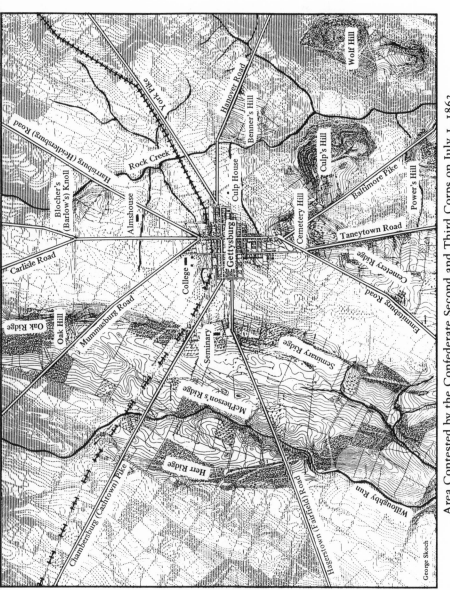

Area Contested by the Confederate Second and Third Corps on July 1, 1863

George Skoch

however, Hill "still could not believe that any portion of the Army of the Potomac was up; and in emphatic words, expressed the hope that it was, as this was the place he wanted it to be." Heth reiterated that he wanted the shoes. "If there is no objection," he said to Hill, "I will take my division to-morrow and go to Gettysburg and get those shoes!" "None in the world," came the nonchalant reply. "A courier was then dispatched with this information to the general commanding," noted Hill in his official report, "and with orders to start Anderson early; also to General Ewell, informing him, and that I intended to advance the next morning and discover what was in my front."[20]

Hill's message to Ewell and Young's postwar recollection indicate that Hill considered Heth's movement on July 1 a reconnaissance in force. Young's account might also be construed to mean that Hill hoped to find the Federals at a disadvantage so that he could strike a blow; however, Heth stated categorically after the war that his chief stressed the importance of not precipitating an engagement. Whatever Hill's full intention, he ordered Pender to support Heth while he awaited Anderson in Cashtown.[21]

When Heth's division took the pike eastward from Cashtown just after daylight on July 1, Hill lay at his headquarters contending with an unknown malady.[22] Heth collided with Buford's cavalry about 8:00 A.M. and soon committed two brigades. The fighting swelled rapidly as Confederate artillery went into action. Back at Cashtown, Hill listened to the distant rumble and discussed its import with Lee, who had arrived shortly after the battle commenced. Hill informed Lee that Heth's instructions called for him to report the presence of any Union infantry immediately "without forcing an engagement."[23] After a short conversation with his chief, Hill rode to the front, where he arrived about noon to find that Heth had stirred a hornet's nest of Union cavalry and infantry and withdrawn to a position on Herr Ridge west of Willoughby Run. Lee joined Hill before long, and shortly after 2:00 P.M. the two men watched an artillery duel between Hill's guns and those of the Federal First Corps east of Willoughby Run.[24]

Once Lee was on the field, responsibility for the battle passed to him. In his postwar memoirs, Walter H. Taylor of Lee's staff wrote that when Lee reached the battlefield he "ascertained that the enemy's infantry and artillery were present in considerable force. Heth's division was already hotly engaged, and it was soon evident that a serious engagement could not be avoided." Actually, at that juncture only the infantry brigades of James J. Archer and Joseph Davis in Heth's division had seen serious action. The Army of Northern Virginia had thus not been drawn into a general battle, and it was Lee rather than Hill who subsequently decided when the other brigades of Heth's division and Pender's division would be sent forward.[25]

In sum, the charge that Hill brought on a major battle against Lee's orders simply does not hold up under careful scrutiny. He did approve a heavy reconnaissance in force for the morning of July 1—a movement that would have been unthinkable had Jeb Stuart been performing his duties. The need for such an action certainly is open to debate; however, Hill informed Lee and Ewell of his intentions, cautioned Heth to be careful, and arranged for Pender to be within supporting distance of Heth. Had Lee wished for Hill to exercise more restraint, he could have communicated with him on the night of June 30. He chose not to do so; neither did he shrink from battle when the tactical situation seemed propitious on July 1. Stuart's absence set in motion the sequence of events that erupted in fighting on July 1, and Lee gave the orders that turned a meeting engagement into a full-scale battle.

What of Hill's responsibility for failing to press the Southern assault late in the afternoon? Between 3:00 and 4:30 P.M., Heth's division and three brigades of Pender's division, together with Rodes's division on their left, forced the Federal First Corps toward Gettysburg and finally to Cemetery Hill. To the northeast, Jubal Early's division of the Second Corps enjoyed similar success against the Union Eleventh Corps. Fortune had guided Lee's infantry to the battlefield in precisely the right places to achieve tactical success; now, as he watched the Union retreat from atop Seminary Ridge, Lee sensed a great

opportunity if the Army of Northern Virginia took the high
ground below Gettysburg. Still hamstrung by a lack of intelligence concerning the enemy's location and strength, however,
he worried about "exposing the four divisions present, already
weakened and exhausted by a long and bloody struggle, to overwhelming numbers of fresh troops."[26]

Hill and Lee were together on Seminary Ridge about 4:30
P.M. Some four hours of daylight remained. Despite his
vaunted reputation as an offensive fighter, Hill evinced little
enthusiasm for renewed assaults on his front. He told Colonel
A. J. L. Fremantle, a British observer, that the Federals had
fought with unusual determination all day. Heth had been
wounded, many field officers were down, and casualties in
some units approached critical levels. "Under the impression
that the enemy were entirely routed," noted Hill in his official
report, "[and with] my own two divisions exhausted by some
six hours' hard fighting, prudence led me to be content with
what had been gained, and not push forward troops exhausted
and necessarily disordered, probably to encounter fresh troops
of the enemy."[27] Hill undoubtedly shared these views with
Lee, who had seen with his own eyes the condition of Hill's
men. Apparently persuaded that no more could be expected of
Heth's and Pender's divisions, Lee turned his attention to
Ewell's corps.

Neither Lee's allusion to "four divisions present" nor Hill's
description of his "exhausted" divisions acknowledged the
presence near the battlefield of R. H. Anderson's five brigades.
Third Corps surgeon Welch wrote about a month after the
battle that Heth and Pender "should have been immediately
reinforced by Anderson with his fresh troops." Colonel Abner
Perrin, who led a brigade in Pender's division, complained bitterly to Governor Luke Bonham of South Carolina on July 29,
1863, that Anderson's division (the largest in the Third Corps)
took no part in the action on the afternoon of July 1. Whether
Anderson or Hill was to blame, conceded Perrin, he could not
say, but he considered this to be *the cause of the failure of the
campaign.*" Captain Young of Pettigrew's brigade related a conversation with Anderson after the war in which the latter

stated that Lee ordered his division to halt some two miles west of Gettysburg. Puzzled by these instructions when sounds of heavy fighting were audible nearby, Anderson sought out Lee for clarification. "General Lee replied that there was no mistake made," Anderson told Young, "and explained that his army was not all up, that he was in ignorance as to the force of the enemy in front, that . . . [Anderson's] alone of the troops present, had not been engaged, and that a reserve in case of disaster, was necessary."[28]

Hill and Lee both knew of Anderson's presence. Hill also must have known that James H. Lane's and Edward L. Thomas's brigades of Pender's division had suffered relatively light casualties. Together these troops likely could have mounted a strong assault in the available daylight. Why did Hill choose not to advocate their deployment for another attack? Perhaps Lee had told him he considered Anderson's division a reserve. Or, as William Woods Hassler has suggested, Hill may have thought that "since [he] and Lee were together . . . it was up to Lee to decide whether Anderson's division should be employed."[29] Whatever the explanation, Lee's presence on Seminary Ridge and knowledge of the pertinent facts rendered him rather than Hill primarily responsible for the decision not to press the Federals along Hill's front after 4:30 P.M.

Hill's withdrawal from the fighting shifted the spotlight to Richard S. Ewell. Before the death of Jackson, Ewell had served only briefly under Lee. The commanding general knew that soldiers in the Second Corps liked and respected "Old Bald Head" and may have heard rumors that on his deathbed Jackson expressed a preference for Ewell as his successor.[30] Convinced that Ewell had recovered from the loss of a leg at Groveton the previous August, Lee settled on him to receive a revamped Second Corps containing Ewell's old division, under Jubal A. Early, the division once commanded by Jackson himself, now under Edward "Allegheny" Johnson, and Robert E. Rodes's division, formerly directed by D. H. Hill. In sending Ewell's name to Jefferson Davis for promotion to lieutenant general, Lee termed him "an honest, brave soldier, who has

Lieutenant General Richard Stoddert Ewell.
(Courtesy of the Library of Congress)

always done his duty well"—far fainter praise than that accorded Hill in the same letter. He sent Ewell's name forward,
said Lee to Colonel Allan after the war, with full knowledge of
"his faults as a military leader—his quick alternations from
elation to despondency[,] his want of decision &c." Lee talked
frankly with Ewell when he made him a lieutenant general,
stressing that as a corps commander Ewell would have to exercise independent judgment. As the army embarked on the
Gettysburg campaign, Lee remarked to Allan, he hoped Ewell
no longer needed minute supervision.[31]

As with Hill, Ewell's first moment of truth as a corps chief
came on July 1. Recalled from his advance against Harrisburg
on June 29, he placed his divisions on roads whence they
might march toward Chambersburg. The next day another directive named Gettysburg as the point of concentration. By
that time, Johnson's division was well on the road to Chambersburg. On the morning of July 1, Rodes's division was a few
miles north of Gettysburg at Heidlersburg, and Early's brigades
were some three miles east of Rodes. Allegheny Johnson's division was far to the west, just outside Chambersburg near
Scotland. Ewell's orders for July 1 permitted him to march to
Cashtown or Gettysburg. When Hill informed Ewell on the
morning of July 1 that Heth was moving toward Gettysburg,
Ewell instructed Rodes and Early to march there as well. "I notified the general commanding of my movements," wrote
Ewell in his official report, "and was informed by him that, in
case we found the enemy's force very large, he did not want a
general engagement brought on till the rest of the army came
up." By the time Lee's message reached him sometime after
noon, Ewell knew that Hill's corps was in a fight. Indeed, some
of Rodes's artillery had reached Oak Ridge and opened on the
Federals in Hill's front. "It was too late to avoid an engagement
without abandoning the position already taken up," Ewell later
explained, "and I determined to push the attack vigorously."[32]

Rodes's infantry went into action against the Union First
Corps north and northwest of Gettysburg shortly after 2:30
P.M., followed by Early's division, which approached from the
north and northeast and struck the Union Eleventh Corps

about an hour later. Outnumbered Federals offered stiff resistance for a time, then fell back to Cemetery Hill in the face of relentless Confederate pressure. Several thousand prisoners and some artillery fell into Southern hands as Ewell's triumphant infantry surged into Gettysburg. Ewell's decision to press the attack after receiving Lee's cautionary orders had been vindicated. To the west, Hill's brigades also had advanced and taken position on Seminary Ridge. It was between 4:30 and 5:00 P.M. Ewell's critics would insist that he lost a fabulous opportunity during the next hour—the time when Hancock later told Fitzhugh Lee that the Federals were vulnerable on Cemetery Hill.[33]

Perhaps the most meticulous account of Ewell's movements after he entered Gettysburg came from the pen of Campbell Brown. As Ewell's stepson and staff officer, Brown had direct knowledge of the events. It is true that by the time he wrote in December 1869, he believed that his stepfather had been wronged by those who said he vacillated at the decisive moment. Nonetheless, his version of what transpired accords with most of the known facts. "I shall set down facts as well & truly as I can," he wrote, "remembering them more distinctly because [they were] discussed & seem[ed] to be important at the time & soon after."[34]

Brown met Ewell as the latter entered Gettysburg amid the divisions of Rodes and Early, which "were mingling in their advance." Early soon appeared and joined Ewell. Riding forward, they "surveyed the ground & examined the position & force on Cemetery Hill. Having concluded to attack, if Hill concurred, Gen'l Ewell ordered Early & Rodes to get ready." Just then a messenger arrived from William "Extra Billy" Smith, one of Early's brigadiers, with news of Federals in the Southern left rear. Early doubted the accuracy of this intelligence but suggested that he suspend his movements long enough to make certain the flank was secure. Ewell told him to do so. "Meantime I shall get Rodes into position & communicate with Hill."[35]

A staff officer galloped in search of Hill, eventually returning with word that he had not advanced against Cemetery Hill and that Lee, who was with Hill on Seminary Ridge, "left it to

Gen'l Ewell's discretion, whether to advance alone or not."
The enemy on the high ground looked formidable, continued
Brown; any assault would entail moving Rodes's and Early's divisions around either end of town and reuniting them in the
open ground in front of Cemetery Hill. There the troops would
be "within easy cannon shot & in open view of an enemy superior in numbers & advantageously posted." Hill clearly intended to offer no support, and Johnson's division had not yet
reached the battlefield. Moreover, Rodes reported that just
three of his brigades were in good condition, while Early also
had just three within easy distance.

"It was, as I have always understood, with the express con-
currence of both Rodes & Early," concluded Brown, "& largely
in consequence of the inactivity of the troops under Gen'l
Lee's own eye . . . that Gen'l Ewell finally decided to make no
direct attack, but to wait for Johnson's coming up & with his
fresh troops seize & hold the high peak [Culp's Hill] to our left
of Cemetery Hill." The notion that Ewell's decision lost the
battle was, in Brown's opinion, "one of those frequently recur-
ring but tardy strokes of military genius, of which one hears
long after the minute circumstances that rendered them at the
time impracticable, are forgotten."

Brown's narrative has no mention of dramatic confronta-
tions with Trimble or Gordon. Early and Ewell are the principals, and it is thus instructive that Early's official report agrees
in essentials with Brown. As he rode into town in the wake of
retreating Federals, Early took in a chaotic scene. Ahead, to the
south, loomed Cemetery Hill, presenting a "very rugged as-
cent" and defended by enemy artillery that disputed the Confederate advance. Union prisoners were so numerous as "really
to embarrass" the Southern infantry. Far from a dramatic rout
(as many postwar writers would describe it), the Federal withdrawal, especially to the west, was carried out in "compara-
tively good order." Still, Early believed an immediate advance
would expand on the success already won, and he set out to
find Ewell or Hill.

Before he located either lieutenant general a message arrived
from Extra Billy Smith telling of a Federal threat approaching
on the York road. Early doubted the veracity of this report but

Major General Jubal Anderson Early.
(Courtesy of the Library of Congress)

thought it "proper to send General Gordon with his brigade to take charge of Smith's also, and to keep a lookout on the York road, and stop any further alarm." He also sent word to Hill, by a member of Pender's staff he met in the town, that "if he [Hill] would send up a division, we could take the hill to which the enemy had retreated." Shortly thereafter, Early found Ewell, conveyed his views, and was "informed that Johnson's division was coming up, and it was determined with this division to get possession of a wooded hill to the left of Cemetery Hill, which it commanded."[36]

Both Brown's and Early's accounts suggest that Ewell and Early discussed the situation and concluded that a successful assault against Cemetery Hill would require help from A. P. Hill; failing in that, Culp's Hill should be the target once Allegheny Johnson's division arrived.

Robert Rodes's report provides additional information relating to the situation about 4:30 P.M. Even before the Federals had been cleared from Gettysburg, asserted Rodes, "the enemy had begun to establish a line of battle on the heights back of the town, and by the time my line was in a condition to renew the attack, he displayed quite a formidable line of infantry and artillery immediately in my front, extending smartly to my right, and as far as I could see to my left, in front of Early." To have assaulted that line with his division, which had suffered more than twenty-five hundred casualties, "would have been absurd." With no Confederates in evidence on Rodes's right— where Hill's corps held the Southern line—and no specific orders to continue the advance, Rodes assumed that Lee's previous instructions to avoid a general engagement still held and began to place his troops in a defensive posture.[37] Brown's observation that Ewell instructed Rodes to "get ready" to advance does not necessarily contradict Rodes's statement that he received no "specific orders" to do so. The divisional leader might well have received an initial directive to prepare his men, concluding later, when no follow-up order came, that there would be no renewal of the assault.

Three last pieces of evidence suggest that the Federals presented a daunting front along Cemetery Hill as soon as the

Confederates took possession of Gettysburg. Ewell's own report mentioned that the "enemy had fallen back to a commanding position known as Cemetery Hill, south of Gettysburg, and quickly showed a formidable front there." Moreover, an absence of favorable positions for artillery prevented Ewell's bringing artillery to bear on the Federals. Second Corps topographer Jedediah Hotchkiss's entry in his journal for July 1 noted "complete success on our part": "The pursuit was checked by the lateness of the hour and the position the enemy had secured in a cemetery." Even John Gordon offered testimony radically at odds with his postwar posturing. In a letter to his wife written six days after the fighting, Gordon observed that his brigade "drove [the Federals] before us in perfect confusion; but night came on [and] they fell back to a strong position & fortified themselves."[38]

While James Power Smith of Ewell's staff rode in search of Lee and Ewell and his subordinates continued to gather the scattered Second Corps units, the commanding general had sent Walter Taylor to find Ewell. The two messengers undoubtedly passed each other somewhere on the field. Taylor soon reached Ewell with word that Lee had "witnessed the flight of the Federals through Gettysburg and up the hills beyond. . . . It was only necessary to press 'those people' in order to secure possession of the heights, and that, if possible, he wished him to do this." Ewell expressed no objection, remembered Taylor after the war, thereby conveying the impression that he would seek to implement Lee's order. "In the exercise of that discretion, however, which General Lee was accustomed to accord to his lieutenants," added Taylor, "and probably because of an undue regard for his admonition, given early in the day, not to precipitate a general engagement, General Ewell deemed it unwise to make the pursuit. The troops were not moved forward, and the enemy proceeded to occupy and fortify the position which it was designed that General Ewell should seize."[39]

Taylor's account is notable for its distortion of the conditions on Ewell's end of the field. It described a Federal "flight" when most of the Union troops maintained some order to their lines; it claimed that Ewell failed to execute Lee's order to take the heights when Lee had only suggested an attack against the high ground if the situation seemed favorable; and it spoke of Federals "occupying and fortifying ground" as a result of Ewell's dereliction that they already held and were fortifying. Overall, Taylor's narrative illustrates nicely the degree to which officers not present on the Confederate left, including Lee in his postwar statements, minimized the obstacles faced by Ewell and exaggerated the Second Corps chief's indecision.

Ewell confronted a very difficult choice on the late afternoon of July 1. Lee manifestly wished for him to capture Cemetery Hill. Accomplishment of this object would have entailed not a continuation of the previous assaults, as so many of Ewell's critics blithely claimed, but the preparation and mounting of an entirely new assault using portions of Rodes's and Early's divisions. With enough time to gather the troops and stage them south of town, Ewell might have brought to bear six brigades—at most six to seven thousand men. Numerous factors militated against a rapid deployment of such a striking force: the streets of Gettysburg were clogged with men, and units were intermixed; the soldiers were tired after a long day of marching and fighting; thousands of Union prisoners demanded attention; Extra Billy Smith's warning of Federals on the York pike and later cavalry reports of menacing Union troops were potentially ominous. Most important, Union strength on the heights was unknown, though clearly growing, and Allegheny Johnson's division had yet to reach a position from which it might support an assault.

Douglas Southall Freeman wrote that Ewell could not reach a decision. But Ewell did reach a decision—not to attack Cemetery Hill. Although it was not the decision that Lee wished him to make, it certainly was reasonable given the situation. All of which does not prove Ewell experienced no loss of nerve that eventful afternoon. Perhaps he did. Perhaps, as Lee and other critics of Ewell later suggested, the general's old inability to function without specific orders paralyzed him. If that was the case, Lee must shoulder much of the responsibility for Ewell's failure. For if, as he told Colonel Allan after the war, Lee knew that Ewell lacked decisiveness, he should have applied a stronger hand. Lee realized that Ewell was not Jackson or Longstreet and should have modified his method of command accordingly. If he issued a discretionary order when he really wanted to convey a desire that Ewell take those heights (as Taylor's testimony implied), Lee should have known that an indecisive Ewell might react as he did. Direct instructions would have avoided any confusion.

Both A. P. Hill and Richard S. Ewell have suffered more than a century's carping about their conduct on July 1, 1863. Neither of them performed brilliantly; each worked in the immense shadow of Stonewall Jackson, whose greatest triumph remained vividly present in the minds of their fellow soldiers in the Army of Northern Virginia. Hill did not cause the battle to be fought, nor did he or Ewell cost the South a more impressive victory. At every crucial moment, Lee was on the field and able to manage events. In the end, he more than any of his lieutenants controlled the first day's action. Anyone seeking to apportion responsibility for what transpired on the Confederate side on the opening day at Gettysburg should look first to the commanding general.

From Chancellorsville to Cemetery Hill

O. O. Howard and Eleventh Corps Leadership

A. WILSON GREENE

aptain Frederick Otto von Fritsch spoke for many of his comrades in characterizing the Battle of Chancellorsville. "On the sixth day of May orders came for the Eleventh Corps to march to United States Ford to recross the Rappahannock River on pontoon bridges . . . and to march back to the old camps," wrote von Fritsch. "I recrossed with a heavy heart, and . . . I felt tears rolling down my cheeks. I was ashamed of this battle, and deplored the sad experience of the Eleventh Corps." "The army, at least our corps, is demoralized," concurred Frederick C. Winkler of the 26th Wisconsin. "Officers talk of resigning and a spirit of depression and lack of confidence manifests itself everywhere." Major General Oliver Otis Howard, the Eleventh Corps commander, agreed that "there was no gloomier period during our great war than the month which followed the disasters at Chancellorsville."[1]

A combination of factors made that month grim for the unlucky Eleventh, the most prominent of which was a negative perception of the outfit's performance on May 2, 1863. A portion of "Stonewall" Jackson's command had driven the Eleventh from its vulnerable position on the right flank of the Army of the Potomac in an action more tactically and logistically impressive than strategically decisive. The corps had generally acquitted itself well in a nearly hopeless situation and delayed Confederate progress until dark. Four days later, the Union forces retreated to Stafford County in ignominious defeat, and the army and the press began to search for culpable parties.[2]

The burden of responsibility for the disaster at Chancellorsville settled quickly, if unjustly, on the Eleventh Corps. Nearly
50 percent of the unit hailed from Germany, and this ethnic
composition made the entire corps a natural target for per-
secution. "The troubles of the corps arose," wrote historian
Edwin B. Coddington, "from the prejudice of the Americans
and the defensive attitude of the Germans." Well might the
German-Americans and their compatriots who wore the crescent badge of the Eleventh Corps bridle when greeted in camp
by cruel jokes calculated to humiliate and offend. "[You] fights
mit Sigel but runs mit Schurz, you tam cowards," ran the typical refrain.[3] The effects of such bigotry were exacerbated because many veterans of George B. McClellan's time as army
commander refused to accept the Eleventh Corps as a merito-
rious member of the Army of the Potomac (they identified the
Eleventh with John Pope's Army of Virginia), an attitude that
contributed to their propensity for scorn.[4]

Northern journalists carried this theme to all corners of the
country. Many newspapers spoke of the "unexampled mis-
conduct" of the Eleventh Corps and how "the whole failure of
the Army of the Potomac was owing to [its] scandalous pol-
troonery." Such criticism, particularly when without foundation in fact, had a predictably ill effect on the men in question.[5]

A brigade commander in the Eleventh Corps approached his
superior after Chancellorsville with an unmistakable message:

> The officers and men of this brigade . . . filled with indignation,
> come to me, with newspapers in their hands, and ask if such be
> the reward they may expect for the sufferings they have endured
> and the bravery they have displayed. . . . It would seem as if a
> nest of vipers had but waited for an auspicious moment to spit
> out their poisonous slanders upon this heretofore honored
> corps. . . . I have been proud to command the brave men in this
> brigade; but I am sure that unless these infamous falsehoods be
> retracted and reparation made, their good-will and soldierly
> spirits will be broken. . . . I demand that the miserable penny-
> a-liners who have slandered the division, be excluded . . . from
> our lines, and that the names of the originators of these slanders

be made known to me and my brigade, that they may be held responsible for their acts.[6]

Major General Carl Schurz, the recipient of this petition, expressed his concerns to Joseph Hooker, the commander of the Army of the Potomac, in a May 9 communique. "I would . . . respectfully observe," stated Schurz, "that the measureless abuse and insult which is heaped upon the Eleventh Corps by the whole army and the press, produces a state of mind among the soldiers, which is apt to demoralize them more than a defeat."[7] Schurz sought to publish his Chancellorsville report to relieve the corps of its odious stigma. When this effort failed, he printed a letter in the *New York Times* demanding an immediate congressional investigation, a request that also fell on deaf ears. Schurz concluded that "a scapegoat was wanted for the remarkable blunders which had caused the failure of the Chancellorsville Campaign," and the Eleventh Corps fit the bill.[8]

As a result, the corps seethed with resentment in mid-May 1863. General Howard did little to mitigate the bruised egos of his troops, accepting practically no personal responsibility for the debacle on May 2. His attitude aggravated ill feelings among German soldiers already upset that Howard had replaced the immensely popular Franz Sigel in late March. "It is said that General Sigel is coming back to the Army of the Potomac to have an enlarged command, his old corps included," wrote a Wisconsin soldier on May 11. "I hope it is so. He is the man to command this corps, all have confidence in him, while very little confidence is felt in General Howard." Charles Wickesburg of the 26th Wisconsin spoke in more extreme terms: "In time the truth will come out," he observed. "It was all General Howard's fault. He is a Yankee, and that is why he wanted to have us slaughtered, because most of us are Germans. He better not come into the thick of battle a second time, then he won't escape."[9]

Sigel had resigned on February 12 and been replaced temporarily by officers of German extraction promoted from within the corps.[10] Howard, a deeply religious abolitionist from

Major General Oliver Otis Howard.
(Miller's *Photographic History of the Civil War*)

Maine, came from the Second Corps and had compiled a creditable combat record as a brigade and division commander. The New Englander's pious personality won scant favor among soldiers of the Eleventh Corps, who apparently paid minimal attention to their new chief's martial abilities. "Tracts now, instead of sauerkraut," complained the soldiers, who disliked Howard's emphasis on Christian warfare. Had Republicans in Maine convinced Howard to run for governor in early June, most members of the corps would have been happy to see him go.[11]

Howard's command consisted of three divisions. Brigadier General Francis Channing Barlow, who replaced the wounded Charles Devens, Jr., after Chancellorsville, led the two brigades of the first division. Slender, pale, beardless, and not yet thirty years old, Barlow was a Harvard graduate and New York lawyer who had demonstrated bravery under fire on the Peninsula and at Antietam.[12] The boyish-looking general ruled his division with a martinet's hand, prompting a member of the 153d Pennsylvania to label his tenure "an epoch in our history, which will never be forgotten by those who had the misfortune to serve under him. As a taskmaster he had no equal. The prospect of a speedy deliverance from the odious yoke of Billy Barlow filled every heart with joy." Barlow reciprocated his men's distrust. "You can imagine my disgust & indignation at the miserable behavior of the 11th Corps," he wrote on May 8. "You know how I have always been down on the 'Dutch' & I do not abate my contempt now." Although not apparent from this statement, the native-born regiments of the corps also attracted Barlow's contempt.[13]

The commander of Barlow's first brigade, Colonel Leopold von Gilsa, learned firsthand about his chief's unforgiving style of leadership. Admired by a comrade as "one of the bravest of men and an uncommonly skillful officer," von Gilsa would be arrested by Barlow during the march to Gettysburg for allowing more than one man at a time to leave ranks to fetch water.[14]

Brigadier General Nathaniel C. McLean led the second brigade of the first division at Chancellorsville, but Howard

Brigadier General Francis Channing Barlow.
(Miller's *Photographic History of the Civil War*)

found McLean's battlefield performance lacking and banished the former Cincinnati lawyer to a staff job in the Ohio Valley. Twenty-seven-year-old Adelbert Ames replaced McLean. Ames had graduated fifth in the West Point class of 1861 and risen to command the 20th Maine. His promotion to brigadier general on May 20, 1863, qualified him as one of the "boy generals" of the Union.[15]

Baron Adolph Wilhelm August Friedrich von Steinwehr continued at the head of the second division after Chancellorsville. This forty-one-year-old scion of an Old World military family came to America in the 1840s seeking a commission in the United States Army. Failing in this, he settled for marriage to an Alabama woman and eventually moved to a farm in Connecticut. One of Pope's division commanders in the Army of Virginia, von Steinwehr impressed a Pennsylvania soldier as "accomplished and competent, and deserv[ing] of more credit than he ever received."[16]

Neither of von Steinwehr's brigade commanders at Chancellorsville retained his post during the Gettysburg campaign. Colonel Adolphus Buschbeck of the first brigade became ill in early June, and Colonel Charles Robert Coster of the 134th New York filled his place. Coster had begun the war as a private; Gettysburg would be his only battle in brigade command. Colonel Orland Smith of the 73d Ohio assumed control of the second brigade, which had been Barlow's at Chancellorsville, and soon won the affection of his men and praise from the difficult Barlow.[17]

The most renowned of Howard's subordinates was Carl Schurz, who led the third division and stood second only to Sigel himself in the estimation of German-Americans. Politics figured more prominently than the military in Schurz's European background, and upon arriving in Wisconsin he had immersed himself in antislavery activities. Lincoln rewarded Schurz for his work in the 1860 presidential canvass with the Spanish portfolio, but in 1862 Schurz returned from Madrid seeking a commission in the army. Lincoln accommodated his influential friend; Schurz responded by displaying some promise in the field. More important, the Germans of the Eleventh

Corps considered him their spiritual leader and a deserving candidate for corps command.[18]

The brigade-level leadership of the third division remained intact after Chancellorsville. Alexander Schimmelfennig, thirty-eight years old and a native of the Prussian province of Lithuania, headed the first brigade. According to an oft-told fable, Lincoln commissioned Schimmelfennig a brigadier general in November 1862 because he found the immigrant's name irresistible. Short, thin, and customarily dressed in old uniforms, Schimmelfennig cut a figure less memorable than his multisyllabic surname. He suffered from chronic dyspepsia, diarrhea, and bad ankles, and as might be imagined, his disposition left something to be desired.[19] Schimmelfennig's counterpart in the third division also had a name most Americans found unpronounceable. Wladimir Krzyzanowski emigrated from Poland in 1846, settling in New York. He organized the 58th New York in 1861 and served in Pope's army as a brigade commander. "Kriz," as he was known in the ranks, proved to be an inspirational officer who led by example.[20]

On balance, the Eleventh Corps possessed a solid stable of officers on the eve of Gettysburg. Schurz, von Gilsa, Schimmelfennig, Krzyzanowski, and von Steinwehr had exhibited reasonably impressive military skills, while Ames and Barlow boasted excellent credentials. The temporary brigade commanders, Smith and Coster, entered the campaign with question marks beside their names, as did Howard, whose experience at Chancellorsville had diminished an otherwise enviable record.[21]

Back in its camps near Brooke Station on the Richmond, Fredericksburg & Potomac Railroad by May 8, the Eleventh Corps began a period of restoration. Efficient logisticians soon replaced the equipment and supplies sacrificed south of the Rappahannock. "This attended to, things began to look more cheerfully," wrote a soldier from Pennsylvania. "The despondency of the men gradually vanished, and soon all traces of our late disaster were obliterated."[22] On June 12 the corps folded its tents and began to follow R. E. Lee's northward-marching

Major General Carl Schurz.
(Miller's *Photographic History of the Civil War*)

Army of Northern Virginia. According to Carl Schurz, the Federals were "ready and eager to march and fight."[23]

The Eleventh Corps evinced that eagerness perhaps more than any other unit in Hooker's army. Its maligned men harbored disappointment, anger, and hostility. Already outsiders in the Army of the Potomac by virtue of their military pedigree and ethnicity, the soldiers of the crescent tramped north hoping for an opportunity to shed their dishonorable post-Chancellorsville reputation. "May we meet Lee somewhere soon," wrote an officer to von Gilsa on June 15, "and may the Eleventh Corps prove that it is as good and brave as any other."[24]

The corps followed a route through Hartwood Church and Catlett's Station, where it joined Major General John F. Reynolds's newly constituted right wing of the army. Howard's troops then moved to Manassas, Centreville, and Goose Creek, just south of Leesburg, marching, according to Howard, "in a very orderly style" and obeying his orders "with great alacrity." After barely escaping capture at the hands of John S. Mosby's cavalry, Howard left Goose Creek on June 24 and crossed the Potomac at Edwards Ferry.[25]

All question of morale disappeared when the corps entered Maryland. The verdant countryside and warm greetings from loyal citizens invigorated the soldiers. Lieutenant Albert Wallber of the 26th Wisconsin vividly recalled June 24: "Having tramped around northern Virginia . . . and viewed nothing but those melancholy pine forests, barren, impoverished fields . . . and old dilapidated homes . . . where a deathlike stillness prevailed," wrote Lieutenant Wallber, "our feelings may be imagined when we stepped on Maryland's shore and beheld the fertile fields, rich pastures, [and] well-kept gardens . . . all showing the prosperity of the inhabitants. The contrast between the two shores was so conspicuous that we really feasted on the landscape." "What a sudden change had overcome the men!" exclaimed a member of the 153d Pennsylvania. "How easy their steps and how cheerful their countenances." A soldier in the 33d Massachusetts gave similar testimony on June 27, writing that the "fate of Maryland and Washington is about to be decided. . . . Our boys have fought well heretofore and we believe that they will now fight better than ever."[26]

George G. Meade's ascension to command of the army on June 28 had a positive, if muted, effect on the leaders of the Eleventh Corps. Howard considered Hooker to be morally impure, and his distrust of "Fighting Joe" had deepened when he learned that Hooker held the Eleventh Corps responsible for the defeat at Chancellorsville. Schurz testified that the army was pleased with Meade's appointment because "everybody respected him." Captain Alfred E. Lee of the 82d Ohio recognized that a change in command on the eve of battle had potentially serious implications for morale: "But fortunately, a feeling had taken hold of the army that it had suffered disasters enough, and that the time had now come whatever leader and at whatever cost. This sentiment fired every breast and reduced the matter of change of commanders to the dimensions of a mere passing incident."[27]

On June 29, the Eleventh Corps entered Emmitsburg, Maryland, a village near the Pennsylvania border. As the corps made camp, the soldiers knew that a major battle loomed on the horizon, but their attitude had come full circle since May 6. "General Lee had advertised that his 'troupe' will perform in Pennsylvania for a short time," wrote a man in the 33d Massachusetts, "but I think he will have to dance to just such tunes as we see fit to play for him." According to Lieutenant Colonel Edward Salomon of the 82d Illinois, "every man felt that . . . a complete victory here meant the beginning of the end of the Rebellion."[28]

After a march of nearly twenty miles over muddy roads on the twenty-ninth, the Eleventh Corps rested around St. Joseph's College near Emmitsburg. Howard ordered his troops to move a short distance northwest of the town on June 30, a day that otherwise provided the men a welcome respite from marching. Howard, Schurz, and other officers found comfortable lodging at the college, which they variously described as a nunnery or seminary.[29]

Meade assigned the left wing of the army, composed of the First, Third, and Eleventh corps, to Reynolds on June 30. That

concern about where best to deploy his men prompted Howard to ride first to Seminary Ridge and then back across the Emmitsburg road to parallel high ground that reached a northern terminus at the town cemetery. Noticing another elevation to the right and recognizing the natural value of the eminence on which he stood, Howard turned to his adjutant general, T. A. Meysenburg, and said, "This seems to be a good position, Colonel." Meysenburg responded, "It is the only position, General."[38]

Some writers credit Reynolds with selecting Cemetery Hill as the anchor for the Union line at Gettysburg. At least one account attributes the decision to von Steinwehr.[39] The evidence seems clear, however, that O. O. Howard was the initial architect of the defensive position that would prove so strong during the next fifty-four hours. Howard himself wrote in 1884 that there "is no official communication or testimony from any quarter whatever . . . which even claims that any orders . . . to occupy Cemetery Hill or Ridge were delivered to me." Captain Hall confirmed that he did find Reynolds, who instructed him to tell Howard to bring the Eleventh Corps forward as rapidly as possible but "gave no order whatever in regard to occupying Cemetery Hill, nor did he make any allusion to it." Hall returned to Howard, encountered him hurrying into Gettysburg, and relayed Reynolds's message. "Riding into the town at your side," stated Hall, "I remember that . . . you pointed to the crest of Cemetery Ridge on our right and said: 'There's the place to fight this battle,' or words to similar effect."[40]

No military genius was required to recognize the obvious defensive qualities of Cemetery Hill. Stone fences formed natural breastworks for infantry; gentle slopes provided outstanding locations for artillery. Culp's Hill and Cemetery Ridge offered strong protection on the flanks, and the position's convex shape would allow reinforcements to move quickly to any point along the line.[41]

Not entirely satisfied with his view of the distant battlefield from Cemetery Hill, Howard rode into town to obtain a better vantage point. He first tried to ascend the belfry of the courthouse but found no ladder or stairway. A young man named

D. A. Skelly directed the general to a building across the street, at the intersection of Baltimore and Middle streets, known as Fahnestock's Observatory. Howard climbed a flight of stairs and emerged onto a small railed balcony from which he and a few staff officers gained a clear view of the surrounding terrain. Employing field glasses and maps, Howard carefully studied the landscape where his men likely would be deployed when they arrived to support the beleaguered First Corps.[42]

While Howard made these observations, a young cavalry officer named George Guinn reported that General Reynolds had been wounded. Moments later, about 11:30 A.M., another officer, perhaps Captain Hall or Major William Riddle of the First Corps, announced that Reynolds had died and that Howard now commanded the field. "Is it confessing weakness to say that when the responsibility of my position flashed upon me I was penetrated with an emotion never experienced before or since?" asked Howard in a postwar account. "My heart was heavy and the situation was grave indeed but I did not hesitate and said: 'God helping us, we will stay here till the army comes.' "[43]

Reynolds's death sent changes rippling through the command of the Eleventh Corps. Schurz succeeded Howard and passed his division to Schimmelfennig, who in turn assigned the first brigade to Colonel George von Amsberg of the 45th New York.[44]

These events at Eleventh Corps headquarters transpired while the rank and file toiled up the highways leading to Gettysburg. In addition to muddy roads and stray wagons from the First Corps, the troops negotiated streams and marshes, climbed fences, and endured drenching thunderstorms during the morning. The skies eventually cleared, but the humidity remained and men unburdened themselves of accoutrements to lighten their loads. Some soldiers in Krzyzanowski's brigade marched barefoot, having worn out their shoes during the march from Brooke Station.[45]

By 10:30 A.M., the division commanders had received Howard's instructions to increase the pace in response to Reynolds's request for help. Schurz read this order while at

Horner's Mill and rode forward to meet Howard. He reached East Cemetery Hill before noon and learned from Howard of Reynolds's demise.[46] The third division, now under Schimmelfennig, arrived in Gettysburg between 12:30 and 1:00 P.M., swinging up the Taneytown road after a rapid march of several miles without a rest. Barlow's division came next, probably thirty minutes later, while von Steinwehr's men labored to join their comrades.[47]

Howard's three divisions numbered fewer than nine thousand effectives, making his command the second smallest corps in the army.[48] Twenty-six guns under Major Thomas W. Osborn supported the infantrymen. Sixteen of Osborn's pieces were Napoleons and the remainder longer-range 3-inch rifles. Lieutenants Bayard Wilkeson and William Wheeler and Captains Hubert Dilger, Lewis Heckman, and Michael Wiedrich commanded Osborn's batteries.[49]

Upon learning of his ascension to overall command, Howard had returned to Cemetery Hill and established army headquarters. He notified Major General Daniel E. Sickles, chief of the Third Corps, of the situation and urged him to move his troops from near Emmitsburg to Gettysburg as expeditiously as possible. A similar message went to Twelfth Corps commander Major General Henry W. Slocum at Two Taverns near Taneytown, and a summary of events soon was on its way to General Meade. Howard then made a series of decisions based on the realization that he must rely for a time on the troops at hand— decisions that form the crux of the debate over Eleventh Corps leadership on July 1. He responded initially to information supplied by Brigadier General Abner Doubleday, Reynolds's replacement at the head of the First Corps, that the Union right flank west of Gettysburg faced great danger. Schurz should take the first and third divisions, instructed Howard, "to seize and hold a prominent height on the right of the Cashtown road and on the prolongation of Seminary Ridge," an eminence known as Oak Hill.[50]

Two problems rendered these orders obsolete almost immediately. Howard and Reynolds had learned the night before that a portion of the Confederate army had appeared north of Gettysburg at Heidlersburg and that a Rebel division had crossed the mountains at Carlisle. It thus could not have surprised Howard when Brigadier General John Buford of the cavalry reported at 12:30 P.M. that gray-clad units were massing three or four miles north of Gettysburg between the York and Carlisle roads.[51] Howard sent modified orders for Schurz "to halt his command, to prevent his right flank being turned, but to push forward a thick line of skirmishers, to seize the point first indicated [Oak Hill] as a relief and support to the First Corps." As Schurz soon discovered, however, Confederates already had occupied his objective, forcing the Eleventh Corps to form at right angles to Doubleday facing north rather then extending the original Union line.[52]

Several analysts have argued that Howard's decision to advance Schimmelfennig and Barlow north of town sealed the fate of the Eleventh Corps before a Confederate shot had been fired at them. General Howard, wrote one critic, "recognized the fact that the 1st Corps would soon be taken in the flank, and that he would soon be confronted with two confederate army corps. Why he should not at once have withdrawn the 1st corps to Cemetery Ridge, the strength of which he had recognized . . . and there formed his line of battle . . . is not understood." Captain Lee of the 82d Ohio averred that "instead of advancing we should have fallen back as soon as the approach of the enemy from the right was developed . . . with our right well refused upon the town, and our left connecting . . . with the . . . First Corps. We could then have punished the enemy more severely, and, perhaps, have held the town until dark." A staff officer serving with Schurz found Howard culpable not for failing to fall back but for failing to send von Steinwehr to provide direct support for the rest of the corps.[53]

John Reynolds had selected the Union battlefield in the morning, and Doubleday continued to maintain this ground in the early afternoon. "I immediately determined to hold the front line as long as possible," explained Howard, "and when compelled to retreat from the Seminary Line, as I felt I would be, to dispute the ground obstinately; but to have all the time a strong position at the Cemetery . . . that I could hold until at least Slocum and Sickles, with their eighteen thousand rein-forcements, could reach the field."[54]

Edwin B. Coddington assails Howard's reasoning on two counts. First, he argues that Howard was under no obligation to maintain Reynolds's line after the midday lull in the fight-ing and should have withdrawn Doubleday to Seminary Ridge. Second, Coddington terms Howard's reliance on the timely ar-rival of reinforcements "unrealistic."[55]

Even Howard's most severe detractors do not suggest that the First and Eleventh corps had the strength on July 1 to de-feat A. P. Hill and R. S. Ewell on the fields west and north of Gettysburg. Howard's only course was to delay the enemy. Le-gitimate debate, therefore, must revolve around whether Howard most effectively slowed Confederate progress until help arrived from the south (the timing of the arrival of such help is a subject for another inquiry). The Cemetery Hill–Culp's Hill–Cemetery Ridge position clearly offered the best terrain for a tactical defensive. Did Howard do everything pos-sible to secure that ground until the bulk of the Army of the Potomac could reach the field? A review of the evidence sug-gests that his reasons for acting as he did were sound despite the protestations of his critics.

Schurz determined the initial dispositions of the Eleventh Corps. "I ordered General Schimmelfennig . . . to advance briskly through the town, and to deploy on the right of the first corps in two lines," reported the German general. "This order was executed with promptness and spirit." Howard personally accompanied Barlow's division through Gettysburg, beyond which it formed near the Almshouse on Schimmelfennig's right.[56] When the corps appeared on the battlefield, Double-day's men saluted it with ringing cheers.[57]

Schurz had two immediate missions: to protect Doubleday's right and to guard against the anticipated arrival of Confeder-ates from the northeast. To meet these responsibilities, Schurz's line stretched some fifteen hundred yards across the fields north of Gettysburg between the Mummasburg and York roads. A gap of about a quarter-mile separated

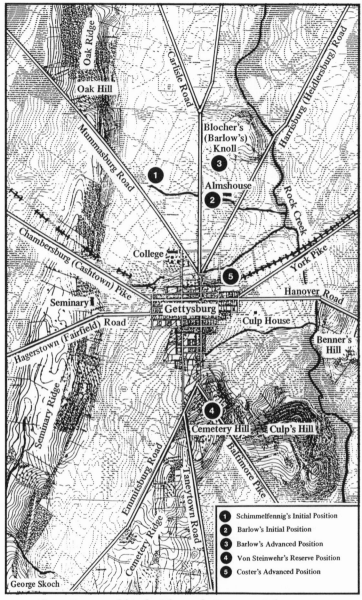

Area Contested by the Eleventh Corps on July 1, 1863

Schimmelfennig's left from Doubleday's right, creating a natural target for attack. Schurz's six thousand soldiers formed the equivalent of a strong skirmish line along their broad front, completing their first dispositions about 2:00 P.M.[58]

At approximately that time, von Steinwehr arrived atop Cemetery Hill, executing Howard's decision to make it the reserve position for the corps. Von Steinwehr placed Coster's brigade on the northeast end of the hill in support of Wiedrich's battery. Smith's brigade moved to the northwest in support of Heckman's guns. The rest of Osborn's artillery had accompanied Schurz—Wilkeson with Barlow, and Dilger and Wheeler with Schimmelfennig.[59]

Howard reported his actions to Meade and repeated his plea for support from Slocum and Sickles about 2:00 P.M. He also ordered his brother to consult with Buford about the approach of Confederates from the north and personally inspected the Eleventh Corps line from right to left. Continuing on to Doubleday's part of the field, Howard found the First Corps commander about a quarter-mile beyond the seminary. After examining the First Corps front, Howard accepted Doubleday's assurance that McPherson's woods would shield the Federal left and told the New Yorker to maintain his position as long as possible before retiring to the designated rallying point on Cemetery Ridge. These instructions were consistent with Howard's strategy of delay; so too was his denial of Doubleday's request for help from von Steinwehr—a movement of troops off of Cemetery Hill, he thought, would compromise the integrity of the Federal reserve.[60]

Shortly after Schurz had deployed the third division, Confederate artillery on Oak Hill began to shell his exposed troops in the valley below. To Schurz's left, Rebel infantry pressed against elements of the First Corps, and Schurz noticed enemy soldiers maneuvering to his front. When the acting corps commander looked to his right, however, he witnessed a more ominous sight. "I had ordered General Barlow to refuse his right wing, that is to place his right brigade, Colonel Gilsa's, a little in the right rear of his other brigade, in order to use it against possible flanking movement by the enemy," observed Schurz.

"But I now noticed that Barlow, be it that he had misunderstood my order, or that he was carried away by the ardor of the conflict, had advanced his whole line and lost connection with my third division on his left, and . . . he had instead of refusing, pushed forward his right brigade, so that it formed a projecting angle with the rest of the line."[61]

Barlow had committed the tactical error that, more than any other Eleventh Corps command decision of the day, dictated the course of combat on that part of the field. Why did he do it? Did he act on his own accord, or did he respond to orders? What potential advantage might have been gained by advancing from the Almshouse line?

The evidence seems conclusive that Barlow made this decision of his own volition.[62] Howard had accompanied him when the first division marched through Gettysburg on its initial deployment, then departed to inspect Schurz's and Doubleday's positions once Barlow halted at the Almshouse. Howard had ordered Barlow and Schimmelfennig to seize Oak Hill; "but as soon as I heard of the approach of Ewell and saw that nothing could prevent the turning of my right flank if Barlow advanced," wrote Howard, "the order was countermanded."[63] The attempt to occupy Oak Hill ended as soon as Schimmelfennig's division reached the ground between the Mummasburg and Carlisle roads and discovered Confederates on the heights. It is thus difficult to ascribe Barlow's advance at 2:30 P.M. to orders that had ceased to apply practically and explicitly more than an hour earlier.

Schurz's postwar writings charitably allow that a misunderstanding of his directive to refuse the right flank might explain Barlow's actions. Schurz made no such allowance, however, in his official report. Barlow informed his mother after the battle that he had "formed as directed," but it is hard to imagine that he could so badly misconstrue an order. Even if he did, his culpability remains. Other testimony portrays Barlow in an aggressive mood. Captain von Fritsch remembered that the general ordered skirmishers toward Blocher's Knoll, a hillock overlooking Rock Creek to Barlow's right front. Shortly thereafter, recalled E. C. Culp of the 25th Ohio, Barlow sent his division to support the skirmishers with the words, "What is that skirmish line stopping for?"[64]

If it may be agreed that Barlow was the author of his division's development, what might have prompted this fatal decision? Blocher's Knoll did rise slightly higher than the ridge occupied by the division near the Almshouse, and its cleared summit offered reasonable positions for artillery. But thick woods began about one hundred feet below the crest toward Rock Creek, severely limiting the field of fire in the direction of the anticipated Confederate advance.[65] Most likely, Barlow saw the unprotected left of Brigadier General George Doles's Georgia brigade, which was maneuvering opposite Schimmelfennig's position, and could not resist the temptation to take Doles in flank and rear.[66]

Caught off guard by the shift on his right, Schurz ordered Schimmelfennig to conform with Barlow's dispositions so as to maintain contact between the first and third divisions. Krzyzanowski's brigade moved out, lengthening the Eleventh Corps line. Schurz also sent couriers to Howard renewing his request that one of von Steinwehr's brigades advance through town and take position on Barlow's right and rear to mitigate the impact of an attack against that exposed flank.[67]

Potential danger became reality about 3:00 P.M. Barlow had moved some twenty-one hundred men on or near Blocher's Knoll when the Federals received fire from Confederate artillery to the northeast along the Harrisburg road. "Then came one of the most warlike and animated spectacles I ever looked upon," stated a Confederate staff officer. "Gordon & Hays charged across the plateau in their front, at double-quick, sweeping everything before them, and scattering the extreme right of the enemy."[68]

In fact, only Brigadier General John B. Gordon's Georgia brigade of fifteen hundred effectives and Doles's fourteen hundred men launched the initial infantry assault against the Eleventh Corps. Doles's presence probably explained why Barlow had advanced northward in the first place. Gordon's appearance, remarkably, came as a surprise. The Federals had known of a Confederate threat from the north since the previous evening;

Rodes's division had occupied Oak Hill and undertaken offensive operations against the right of the First Corps; and the Southern guns along the Harrisburg road had begun to pound Barlow's soldiers. Still, when Gordon's men boiled out of the woods skirting the bed of Rock Creek, they caught the Eleventh Corps unprepared.[69]

Gordon struck Barlow's vulnerable right flank held by von Gilsa's little brigade—the same men who had absorbed Jackson's initial blow on May 2. According to a Confederate participant, "it was a fearful slaughter, the golden wheat fields, a few minutes before in beauty, now gone, and the ground covered with the dead and wounded in blue."[70] When von Gilsa gave way, Gordon focused on the exposed right flank of Ames's brigade. Contending with both Doles and Gordon, Ames's outnumbered troops also collapsed. Barlow attempted to rally his soldiers but fell wounded with a bullet in his left side. Ames assumed command of the division and sought to form a new line near the Almshouse. "We ought to have held the place easily, for I had my entire force at the very point where the attack was made," wrote Barlow shortly after the battle. "But the enemies [sic] skirmishers had hardly attacked us before my men began to run. No fight at all was made."[71]

Most accounts disagree with Barlow. Brigadier General Henry J. Hunt, the Union chief of artillery, portrayed the fight between Barlow and the Georgians as "an obstinate and bloody contest. The fighting here was well-sustained." Private G. W. Nichols of the 61st Georgia reported that the Confederates "advanced with our accustomed yell, but they stood firm until we got near them. They then began to retreat in fine order, shooting at us as they retreated. They were harder to drive than we had ever known them before. . . . Their officers were cheering their men and behaving like heroes and commanders of the 'first water.' " The finest tactical study of this engagement calls it "a bruising, violent struggle."[72]

Krzyzanowski's brigade had not reached Ames's left when Gordon and Doles began their attacks. By the time the troops arrived at the Carlisle road, Barlow's men already were withdrawing. Doles centered his attention on Krzyzanowski, and another fierce combat erupted. "Bullets hummed about our ears like infuriated bees, and in a few minutes the meadow was strewn with . . . the wounded and the dead," testified an Ohio officer. "The combatants approached each other until they were scarcely more than seventy-five yards apart, and the names of battles printed on the Confederate flags might have been read, had there been time to read them."[73]

Both of Krzyzanowski's flanks received enfilading fire, and the brigade fell back across the Carlisle road toward an orchard on the north side of Gettysburg. Most of von Amsberg's brigade manned the skirmish line facing Oak Hill or supported Dilger's and Wheeler's batteries on the Eleventh Corps left; Schimmelfennig thus could send only one regiment to Krzyzanowski's aid. This unit, the 157th New York, bravely advanced toward Doles's right flank but met a tremendous fire and suffered 75 percent casualties.[74]

The entire Union line at Gettysburg faced disaster by 3:20 P.M. As the Confederates renewed their attacks against Doubleday, John Buford informed Meade that in his opinion "there seems to be no directing person," an artless indictment of O. O. Howard.[75]

In fact, Howard, Schurz, and Doubleday did attempt to salvage a situation that had quickly become desperate. All three men needed reinforcements, and each of them requested help. Howard asked again that Slocum hurry the Twelfth Corps forward, while Schurz and Doubleday begged Howard for assistance. Howard authorized Schurz to detach a regiment or two to support Doubleday, an option the beleaguered German lacked the manpower to satisfy.[76] Still hoping for the arrival of one of von Steinwehr's brigades, Schurz enjoyed the only reasonable expectation of aid. Howard would claim that before Barlow's advance he had ordered three regiments from Coster's brigade to occupy the north end of town, but other sources mention no such directive. "I feared the consequences of sparing another man from the cemetery," explained Howard. "It was not time to lose the nucleus for a new line that must soon be formed."[77]

About 3:45 P.M., the tenuous rallying point near the Almshouse collapsed. Gordon's men swept forward despite the best efforts of von Gilsa and Ames, and two fresh Confederate brigades menaced the right of the makeshift line. By this time, Howard had definitely instructed von Steinwehr to dispatch Coster's brigade to cover Schurz's withdrawal.[78]

Coster pulled some eleven hundred men off Cemetery Hill before 3:30 P.M., entered Baltimore Street, and marched through town, leaving one regiment at the railroad depot.[79] The remaining eight hundred soldiers filed through the north side of Gettysburg, receiving artillery fire from Oak Hill and passing the wounded and fugitives from both Federal corps. "I led [the brigade] out of the town," said Schurz, "and ordered it to deploy on the right of the junction of the roads . . . which the enemy was fast approaching." Schurz placed Heckman's Ohio battery on the brigade's left, as Coster's men strode toward the impending maelstrom with perfect order and discipline. John F. Sullivan of the 154th New York believed that had his "regiment been on dress parade it could not have done better."[80]

Unfortunately, some of Coster's troops halted below rising ground that obstructed their field of fire. Before they could adjust their position, the brigades of Brigadier General Harry Hays and Colonel Isaac E. Avery had closed to within two hundred yards. "I shall always remember how the Confederate line of battle looked as it came into full view and started down toward us," wrote Private Charles W. McKay of the 154th New York. "It seemed as though they had a battle flag every few rods, which would indicate that their formation was in solid column."[81]

Coster's men, as much as any other unit in the Eleventh Corps, belied their reputation as demoralized cowards. Fighting against tremendous odds, the blue line held long enough for "the first division to enter the town without being seriously molested on its retreat." "Our fire did good execution," boasted McKay, "and their line was stopped in our front." Heckman's gunners pulled their lanyards 113 times before pressured to withdraw. The fierce engagement lasted only a short time before Coster, whose losses would total 250 killed and wounded and another 300 captured, ordered his men to disengage.[82]

Schimmelfennig's division also fell back, fighting as it went. Schurz reported that his old command retreated toward Gettysburg "in good order, contesting the ground step by step with the greatest firmness."[83]

Coster's brigade contributed significantly to the extrication of the Eleventh Corps north of Gettysburg. Might it have accomplished more had Howard acted on Schurz's requests to move it forward sooner? Did Howard's hesitation ensure dire consequences once the army reached the streets of Gettysburg?

It takes a great leap of faith to argue that Coster's tiny regiments could have saved the first division's vulnerable position at Blocher's Knoll. Had Barlow remained at the Almshouse line, however, and Coster moved up on his right rear as Schurz preferred, the Eleventh Corps might well have held its ground somewhat longer. In Howard's defense, it must be recalled that the Union strategy that afternoon revolved around standing firm on Cemetery Hill until the Third and Twelfth corps came up. To detach one-half of the small reserve holding that key ground and risk it in the open fields north of Gettysburg would have entailed a tremendous gamble promising doubtful dividends.

By 4:00 P.M., Confederate attacks against Doubleday's line and Schurz's left threatened to overrun organized Union resistance west and north of Gettysburg. "If you cannot hold out longer," Howard told Doubleday, "you must fall back to the cemetery." At 4:10 P.M., Howard sent both corps commanders instructions to retire fighting to Cemetery Hill, the First Corps to take position on the left and the Eleventh Corps on the right of the Baltimore Pike. Howard ordered Buford to cover Doubleday's left flank during the withdrawal and sent his brother to urge Slocum yet again to move up to Cemetery Hill.[84]

It is difficult to determine whether von Amsberg's brigade or the right flank of the First Corps gave way first. "We of Robinson's division have a very vivid remembrance of a division of the Eleventh Corps throwing away its guns and manifesting intense anxiety to regain the charming shelter of Cemetery Hill," wrote a veteran of the 12th Massachusetts (of the First Corps).[85] A soldier of the 45th New York stated the case for the Eleventh Corps: "We made preparations to defend the college . . . although we saw the left of the First Corps broken to pieces and pursued by overwhelming numbers of the enemy making for the left of the town."[86]

Conflicting evidence likewise exists regarding the nature of the retreat. Many Confederate accounts support the notion that both Union corps fled the field in disarray.[87] "This is far from the truth," claimed Carl Schurz. "There was no element of dissolution in it." The men of the 33d Massachusetts of Smith's brigade watched from Cemetery Hill as blue-clad soldiers "stubbornly retreated, turning every few rods to fire a volley, facing in every direction." E. C. Culp of the 25th Ohio concluded that "there was no organization as far as I could see. Neither was there any great hurry."[88]

Most witnesses do agree that confusion reigned once the troops reached the confines of Gettysburg. Soldiers from the Eleventh and First corps collided in the narrow streets, some of which were dead ends in more ways than one for unfortunate Federals. "The enemy's brigades poured in like . . . ceaseless . . . waves and threatened to overwhelm . . . all that did not flee before them," remembered a Bay State soldier. Skulkers, stragglers, and the panic-stricken from both corps added to the chaos.[89]

General Schimmelfennig crafted his most enduring Civil War legacy by effecting a hairbreadth escape from capture. Climbing a tall fence while sustaining blows from pursuing Confederates, he played dead until the Rebels passed by, his identity masked by his customary private's garb. He then sought shelter in what has been variously described as a water tank, lumberyard, or woodshed but was most likely a pigsty. There the acting division commander would remain undetected for two more days of battle.[90]

Not all of the Eleventh Corps shared the general's luck. Confederates captured more than fourteen hundred soldiers of the crescent in Gettysburg—a total smaller than the number of killed and wounded suffered by the corps during the afternoon's fighting.[91]

A lack of leadership contributed to the disaster in Gettysburg. Although Schurz and Doubleday "were in front of the town till the last minute, doing everything to inspirit their troops," both Eleventh Corps division commanders were indisposed. Howard remained on Cemetery Hill, where smoke and trees obscured his view of the withdrawal. Moreover, no one had designated specific routes of retreat despite Howard's knowledge that the army eventually would be forced to retire under pressure.[92]

No such lapse marred the effort to rally fugitives on Cemetery Hill. "In whatever shape the troops issued from the town, they were promptly reorganized, each was under the colors of his regiment, and in as good a fighting trim as before," reported Schurz. By 4:30 P.M., Howard had firm command of the situation. An aide from Barlow's staff who reported to the field commander remembered with pride "that interview which, in two or three minutes, taught me what a cool and confident man can do. No hurry, no confusion in his mind."[93]

Smith's two thousand troops supported by Wiedrich's battery of three-inch rifles provided the anchor around which the rest of the Union army would form. A crestfallen von Amsberg reached the heights first; Howard personally positioned his brigade by carrying the corps flag to the designated location. Ames arrived next, reporting, "I have no division: it is all cut to pieces." Howard exhorted him to try to extend the line eastward, and Ames "succeeded better than he had feared." Krzyzanowski, now in charge of the third division, appeared about 4:45 P.M. and placed his soldiers on the left flank of the corps behind a stone wall near the cemetery's gate.[94]

Doubleday's veterans supported the Eleventh Corps left, except for one division that occupied Culp's Hill. Osborn selected advantageous ground for his batteries as they arrived, while Buford's cavalry gamely sought to protect the left flank of the First Corps during the retreat. Some of the troops on Cemetery Hill strengthened their lines by constructing breastworks.[95]

The two Union corps had assumed a formidable defensive posture by 5:00 P.M., one which the Confederates chose not to assault. In Carl Schurz's opinion, Ewell and Hill made wise decisions: "[Our] infantry was indeed reduced by . . . one-half its effective force, but all that was left, was good. . . . It is therefore at least doubtful whether they could have easily captured Cemetery Hill before the arrival of . . . reinforcements on our side."[96] Thus did the combat on July 1 conclude with Howard's soldiers holding fast on the crest of Cemetery Hill.

Although fighting had ended, Howard's performance before nightfall inspired further controversy. Meade had learned of Reynolds's death at 1:00 P.M. and immediately sent Major General Winfield Scott Hancock, commander of the Second Corps, to take control of the field at Gettysburg. Both Howard and Sickles ranked Hancock, but Meade trusted the brave Pennsylvanian more than his other two subordinates. Moreover, General in Chief Henry W. Halleck had specifically granted Meade the authority to elevate anyone he wished to field command, regardless of seniority. Hancock left Taneytown about 1:30 P.M. and reached Cemetery Hill a little before 4:30 P.M. All sources agree that the soldiers responded enthusiastically to the popular officer's appearance, but what transpired between Howard and Hancock is the subject of historical debate.[97]

Captain Eminel P. Halstead of Doubleday's staff witnessed Hancock's arrival. Halstead stated that Hancock sought out Howard, who was sitting alone at the time, and declared that Meade had placed him in overall command: "General Howard woke up a little and replied that he was the senior . . . 'I am aware of that, General, but I have written orders in my pocket from General Meade which I will show you if you wish to see them.' " Howard replied that he did not doubt Hancock's word, adding with a certain illogic, "You can give no orders here while I am here." Hancock accepted this arrangement, agreeing to second any order Howard issued rather than debate military protocol in such an emergency. He also told Howard that Meade had instructed him to select the battleground on which the army would make its stand. "But I think this is the strongest position by nature upon which to fight a battle that I ever saw," said Hancock, "and if it meets your approbation I will select this as the battlefield." Howard observed that he also thought "this a very strong position." "Very well, sir, I select this as the battlefield," stated Hancock, who, according to Halstead, "immediately turned away to rectify our lines."[98]

Howard described this incident no fewer than four times in writings spanning a generation. Nowhere did he mention the exchange quoted by Halstead. Instead, Howard characterized Hancock's role as Meade's "temporary chief of staff" and claimed that Hancock reported himself merely as the army commander's representative on the field—although in his official report Howard confessed that Meade had given Hancock orders "while under the impression that he was my senior." Howard asserted that he told Hancock that "this was no time for talking" and instructed him to deploy troops on the left of the Baltimore Pike; Howard himself would place men on the right of the road. "I noticed that he sent Wadsworth's division, without consulting me . . . to Culp's Hill," wrote Howard, "but as it was just the thing to do, I made no objection."[99]

Hancock mentioned nothing of the conversation with Howard in his official report. After the war, Hancock explained that "as soon as I arrived on the field . . . I rode directly to the crest of the hill where General Howard stood, and said to him that I had been sent by General Meade to take command of all the forces present; that I had written orders to that effect with me, and asked him if he wished to read them." "He replied that he did not," concluded Hancock, "but acquiesced in my assumption of command."[100]

Someone's account of this episode is at variance with the truth, and it would appear that Howard had more reason to misrepresent the record than Hancock or the disinterested Halstead.[101] Without doubt, Meade's lack of confidence wounded Howard, as he made clear later that day.

The real issue is not Howard's effort to save face but how the Howard-Hancock controversy affected Union military leadership on Cemetery Hill. Here the verdict is unanimous. Both officers did their utmost to secure the Federal defense; questions of seniority and authority had no effect on the efficiency of

Union operations. "Howard, in spite of his heart-sore, cooperated so loyally with Hancock that it would have been hard to tell which of the two was the commander and which the subordinate," testified Schurz.[102] What pettiness Howard displayed came primarily from his pen after the war rather than on the battlefield itself.

As the sun disappeared behind Seminary Ridge and South Mountain, Howard received Meade's written orders relieving him of command, presumably the same orders Hancock carried in his pocket that Howard had declined to examine. Deeply "mortified" by this directive, Howard asked Hancock to tell Meade that he had discharged his duties faithfully. At the same time, he officially turned the command over to Slocum, the de facto senior officer, who finally had arrived on Cemetery Hill. Howard expressed his evaluation of the day's fighting in a heartfelt dispatch to Meade later that night:

> I believe I have handled these two corps to-day from a little past 11 until 4, when General H[ancock] assisted me in carrying out orders which I had already issued, as well as any of your corps commanders could have done. . . . [Our] position was not a good one, because both flanks were exposed, and a heavy force approaching from the northern roads rendered it untenable, being already turned, so that I was forced to retire the command to the position now occupied, which I regard as a very strong one. The above has mortified me and will disgrace me. Please inform me frankly if you disapprove of my conduct to-day, that I may know what to do.[103]

The distracted general received an indication of Meade's opinion before dawn on July 2 when the two men and some staff officers examined the army's dispositions south of town. "Well, Howard," asked the army commander, "what do you think; is this the place to fight the battle?" Howard naturally replied that he regarded the position he had chosen as the strongest available. "I am glad to hear you say so," agreed Meade, "for I have already ordered the other corps to concentrate here and it is too late to change."[104]

That night Howard and a few of his staff slept in the gatekeeper's house at the cemetery. What remained of the Eleventh

Corps bedded down among the graves, wrapped in their blankets. "There was a profound stillness in the graveyard," remembered Schurz, "broken by no sound but the breathing of the men . . . the tramp of a horse's foot; and sullen rumblings mysteriously floating on the air from a distance all around."[105]

So ended another bloody day of combat for the Eleventh Corps and its leaders, the second in less than two months in which the corps had been driven from a battlefield. Writers for generations would point to May 2 and July 1, 1863, as twin disgraces for a unit deemed to be the weakest in the Army of the Potomac. Is this image deserved? Does the caricature of General Schimmelfennig hiding in a filthy hog's hovel until all danger had passed typify a cowardice and incompetence of the corps as a whole?

Casualty figures suggest otherwise. The Eleventh Corps lost roughly 2,900 men on July 1, and the number of prisoners exceeded killed and wounded in only four regiments in the first and third divisions.[106] Confederate fire felled every regimental commander in Krzyzanowski's brigade. The 82d Ohio lost 150 of its 258 men; fifteen minutes of savage fighting cost the 75th Pennsylvania more than half its strength. John Gordon called the Federal performance on July 1 "a most obstinate resistance," and a veteran of the 157th New York proclaimed after the war that when any "person brands the Eleventh Corps as a corps of cowards, he is falsifying the record."[107]

Francis Barlow leveled the harshest criticism against the corps in the days following the battle. "These Dutch won't fight," he told a friend in August. "Their officers say so & they say so themselves & they ruin all with whom they come in contact." On July 7, Barlow assured his mother, "This is the last of my connection with the division. . . . I would take a brigade in preference to such a division." Barlow may have revealed a jaundiced perspective in his evaluation when he added, "Except among those on our side who are fighting this war upon anti-slavery grounds, there is not much earnestness nor are there many noble feelings and sentiments involved."[108] Barlow's ill-advised occupation of the knoll that now bears his name lends irony to his fault-finding.

Modern students of the battle point out that the Eleventh Corps suffered 50 percent casualties among its units engaged while inflicting only 14 percent casualties on its opponent.[109] But such statistics do not necessarily demonstrate that the Federals fought less courageously than the soldiers of Ewell's corps. The discrepancy may be explained by the patently hopeless Union position on the afternoon of July 1. This last premise, in turn, raises a different question. If the Eleventh Corps had a forlorn mission on the first day at Gettysburg, could its leadership have done anything to ameliorate the situation?

Apart from Barlow's tactical blunder, an analysis of Eleventh Corps generalship on July 1 boils down to an evaluation of O. O. Howard. Howard wrote his wife on July 16 that at "Gettysburg I am awarded much credit & fear that this excess of praise will excite the unkind criticisms of some of my brother officers." As he predicted, articles soon appeared that took him to task for various indiscretions on the first day's field. A soldier from the 25th Ohio reflected the tenor of the denunciations: "I always blamed Howard for that day's work as well as for our defeat at Chancellorsville, and he ought to be praying today for forgiveness for the lives he sacrificed in these two battles, instead of being a preacher and holding a Major-General's commission." Nevertheless, Congress passed a resolution of thanks dated January 28, 1864, praising Howard for his role in selecting the Union position at Gettysburg.[110]

What conclusions should be drawn regarding Howard's leadership on July 1? Events during the next two days vindicated his choice of the Cemetery Hill–Culp's Hill–Cemetery Ridge line as the Union strong point. "Howard fought the first day's battle from the time Reynolds fell to its close," wrote his brother, "with the purpose and plan of securing Cemetery Ridge as the military position from which the great battle with the whole army should be fought."[111]

Howard's tactical execution is a thornier matter. Writers assail him for locating his headquarters on Cemetery Hill, where his view of the battlefield would be obscured; for declining to withdraw Doubleday's corps to Seminary Ridge during the midday lull in the fighting; for failing to erect extensive breast-works along the Union line; and for neglecting to designate specific routes of march through Gettysburg to eliminate confusion during the retreat. Howard's critics insist that he exercised little tactical control over the battle after the initial deployment, allowed both flanks of the Eleventh Corps to hang suspended in the air, and delayed the advance of von Steinwehr's division north of town until it was too late to stem the Confederate tide.[112]

This impressive list of particulars possesses some merit. A more compact defensive position west and north of Gettysburg would have stood up better to Confederate assaults. Howard's notion of occupying Oak Hill would have strengthened Doubleday's right immeasurably had Rodes not already held that high ground, but it would not have secured the Carlisle and Harrisburg road corridors along which Jubal A. Early's division approached the field. During his early afternoon inspection of the Eleventh Corps, Howard should have eliminated the gap between Schimmelfennig's and Robinson's divisions at the hinge of the Eleventh and First corps. He might have acted on Schurz's suggestion that von Steinwehr advance a brigade in support of Barlow before Gordon launched his attack, but von Steinwehr's entire command could not have redeemed the situation after the first division went forward to Blocher's Knoll. Finally, though circumstances dictated a certain degree of confusion in Gettysburg during the Federal retreat, Howard must bear partial responsibility for the disastrous flight through town that resulted in so many Union prisoners.

Would correction of all these tactical oversights have enabled the Army of the Potomac to hold off the Confederates and conduct an orderly withdrawal through Gettysburg after dark? Few historians think so. But because the Union defense on July 1 contributed to the enemy's inability to occupy key ground south of town, Howard did succeed in achieving his overall objective.[113]

Better generalship might have reduced casualties in the Eleventh Corps, especially the number of missing and captured. Some writers suggest that Howard could have accomplished this by retreating earlier to Cemetery Hill, yet such a maneuver might have cost the Federals their final position. As Carl Schurz asked, "Would not the enemy, if we had retreated . . . even one hour earlier, have been in better condition, and therefore more encouraged to make a determined attack upon the cemetery that afternoon,—and with a better chance of success?" Howard himself summed up the first day's fighting by saying that his troops "did wonders: held the vast army of General Lee in check all day; took up a strong position; fought themselves into it, and kept it for the approaching army of the Potomac to occupy with them, so as to meet the foe with better prospects of victory."[114]

The Eleventh Corps performed with honor on July 1, 1863, and deserves a better reputation. Its soldiers, recovered from the reversals if not the recriminations of Chancellorsville, contributed materially to eventual Northern victory at Gettysburg. Except for the personally courageous Barlow's egregious tactical error, brigade and division commanders, including the maligned Alexander Schimmelfennig, handled their units with skill and gallantry. Although he was in charge of the entire field during most of the day, Oliver Otis Howard's performance remains central to an analysis of Eleventh Corps leadership. Hancock, Slocum, and Meade all endorsed Howard's strategic view of the battle and his choice of ground. Howard's tactical leadership in executing his policy of delay may have been flawed, but no one can gainsay his pivotal contribution to the three-day struggle.

Three Confederate Disasters on Oak Ridge

Failures of Brigade Leadership on the First Day at Gettysburg

ROBERT K. KRICK

Any listing of the most victorious days in the tactical annals of the Army of Northern Virginia must include May 2, 1863, and several days at the end of August 1862. Fredericksburg leaps to mind as a thoroughly triumphant day, but the simplicity and ease of General Ambrose E. Burnside's destruction leaves little room for talk of Confederate prowess. Gettysburg hardly stands high on any register of Southern successes—but July 1, 1863, taken alone, was unquestionably one of the best days Lee's army ever enjoyed. Late that afternoon, as Federals scampered through the town in desperate flight, leaving thousands of casualties behind and losing thousands more as prisoners, their prospects were bleak indeed. Some forty hours later the Northern army would be able to claim an immensely important victory that forever dimmed the memory of the Confederate triumph on July 1.

The newly reorganized Army of Northern Virginia that approached Gettysburg at the end of June 1863 seemed an unlikely candidate for quick and sweeping conquests. It had unbounded confidence in its commander, and it rode the momentum imparted by familiarity with success; but it also had a disturbingly large increment of leaders new to their posts and units new to the army—and it did not have the mighty arm of "Stonewall" Jackson to execute Lee's designs. As fate would have it, the entire command structure of the army component that opened the battle was new to its role: A. P. Hill was in his first combat day as corps commander; Henry Heth in his first battle as division commander; and Joseph R. Davis in his first battle as brigade commander.

Under the circumstances, it is not cause for astonishment that four Confederate brigades suffered dreadful disasters west of Gettysburg on July 1. Three of them came to grief within a small piece of Oak Ridge north of the Chambersburg Pike. Their troubles, which displayed an unhappy mixture of poor leadership, inexperience, and bad luck, serve as a case study of failure in the midst of victory. The remarkable part of the story is that even in the face of the three fiascoes on Oak Ridge, Lee's great victory ultimately developed in that sector of the field. Not surprisingly, the eventual victory was compounded of good leadership, experience, and good luck.

Although he could not have foreseen the trend, Gettysburg was the first of many campaigns in which Lee would find himself obliged to exert an ever-stronger personal control on events at the corps and even the division level. Nearly a year later, in May 1864, deterioration in his support would leave Lee with the virtually impossible task not only of directing the army but also literally commanding each of its three corps in person. As July 1863 dawned, however, Lee doubtless presumed that he would be able to continue, at least to a degree, the laissez-faire form of army command that had proved so spectacularly successful in the Jackson era.

Lee faced his increased burdens at Gettysburg in his worst physical condition of the war. Though now in his fifty-seventh year, the army commander was accustomed to bringing phenomenal endurance to his tasks. That spring, however, an attack had floored Lee so thoroughly that it caused concern around headquarters. Whether or not that ailment was—as has been conjectured—the onset of the angina pectoris that ultimately contributed to his death, he had recovered from the episode by mid-April.[1] No evidence of any affliction hampered Lee at Chancellorsville, and the next notable onset of his visceral discomfort that is of record occurred during the fall of 1863. At Gettysburg, though, the general suffered from a debilitating attack of intestinal upset that certainly impaired his strength and probably reduced his ability to bear the added load that befell him. The oft-quoted source for information about Lee's famous and ill-timed malady was a member of "Jeb" Stuart's staff who could not have seen the army commander until late on the second day at Gettysburg, so whether he was afflicted by July 1 remains uncertain. A Louisiana staff officer reported the etiology of Lee's malady as an overdose of "old Virginia flapjacks. . . . Thin as a wafer and big nearly as a cart wheel . . . served hot with fresh butter and maple molasses and folded and folded, layers thick."[2]

Lee's stalwart right arm near the scene of the opening engagement on Oak Ridge should have been the commander of his new Third Corps, Ambrose Powell Hill. The newly minted lieutenant general had just finished a year as the leader of a splendid division with a solid record. Hill would be mysteriously invisible at Gettysburg and would prove a disappointment as a corps commander, but on July 1 there seemed ample reason to trust him. The unbridled aggressive spirit that had made Hill and his division a terror to the enemy while they were in the employ of Stonewall Jackson did not suit his new role so well. James Johnston Pettigrew's brigade of Heth's division had ventured toward Gettysburg on the last day of June and run afoul of John Buford's seasoned Federal cavalry. When Hill expressed his intention to repeat the process on July 1, Pettigrew sent a member of his staff who had served under Hill around Richmond to warn the corps commander to be prepared for opposition, thinking that the familiar face "might have some weight with him." Hill told his former subordinate that he "could not believe that any portion of the Army of the Potomac was up; and, in emphatic words, expressed the hope that it was, as this was the place we wanted it to be."[3] In that incautious spirit, Hill launched Henry Heth's division down the Chambersburg Pike and into the battle at Gettysburg.

As Henry Heth led the movement to Gettysburg with his division, he faced a number of new challenges. Although he had commanded A. P. Hill's division for a time at Chancellorsville because of wounds suffered by his superiors, Heth had been a major general only since late May and this was his first real ex-

Major General Henry Heth.
(Miller's *Photographic History of the Civil War*)

perience as division commander. He had come to the army quite recently bearing the clear imprimatur of R. E. Lee, who, Heth wrote, "has always been my personal friend."[4]

During February 1863, Lee and Stonewall Jackson exchanged correspondence about criteria for promotion, with Jackson eager to use some judicious weighting on behalf of officers who had fought successfully with him for a long time. Lee rejected that notion firmly, saying that merit alone must apply without any hint of credit for propinquity. General Heth deserved a brigade, and Lee wanted to give him one under Jackson. The lieutenant general eventually acquiesced gracefully in the face of higher authority and wrote hopefully to Lee: "From what you have said respecting General Heth, I have been desirous that he should report for duty."[5]

A strong tradition that reveals Lee's high regard for Heth states that the young officer was the only one of his generals— some two hundred of them, first and last—"whom Lee called by his first name." The army commander's regard cannot have been based on any substantive achievements by Heth, whose antebellum career and war experiences had been similarly unremarkable. Conventional wisdom suggested that Heth was an officer dogged by bad luck.[6]

Before he fell prey to bad Civil War luck, Heth had suffered the stigmata of honestly earned bad grades at the United States Military Academy. During his first year at West Point, the young Virginian somehow managed to finish ahead of seven of his forty-five passing comrades. The next year he plummeted to dead last in his class, however, and he clung tenaciously to that rung all the way to graduation. Heth's thirty-seven classmates who graduated ahead of him in 1847 included close friends A. P. Hill, who ranked fifteenth, and Ambrose E. Burnside, who ranked eighteenth. In conduct—which was rated across all four classes—Heth stood 198th out of 218 cadets; Burnside's demerit total was even worse and Hill's barely better.[7]

The young army officer's prewar experience in the old army was as generally quiet as that of hundreds of other West Point graduates in the peacetime establishment. He performed credibly in an 1855 fight with Sioux Indians but enjoyed particular distinction because of his interest in marksmanship systems for both muskets and rifles. While the army and most of its leaders ignored the need for accuracy with shoulder arms and some officers even ridiculed the concept as corrupting the principles of volley firing, Henry Heth methodically translated French marksmanship texts and gathered information on the most successful systems. The War Department eventually accepted the manual that Heth had prepared, and it was published in 1858. The author included a self-deprecating introduction insisting that he could claim no credit for anything new, offering only "a digest of what has already been practised." The U.S. War Department did Heth the honor of reprinting the manual in 1862, identical down to cover color and illustration—but, of course, wiping the rebel's name off the cover and substituting Edwin M. Stanton's suitably patriotic name on an inner page as sponsor.[8]

For most of the war's first two years Heth served in western Virginia. The same tangled mountain terrain and shifting loyalties that had bedeviled R. E. Lee in that region in 1861 frustrated most of Heth's efforts. Confederates in the mountains hoped for great things from the professional soldier sent to lead them and suffered proportionate dismay when affairs continued to be uneasy and confused. On May 23, 1862—the same day that Stonewall Jackson was winning a famous victory in the Shenandoah Valley—Heth launched a surprise attack on Federals under George Crook at Lewisburg. The raw Confederate troops could not execute the apparently sound plan their general put into operation, and they suffered a bitter defeat in consequence. A century later one historian wrote that in that region, "even today you can find people who blame him for the failure to recapture the town." A young girl who lived in Lewisburg at the time recorded with wry amusement the general's fall from grace in local eyes: "Up to this time my father had been much struck with General Heth's resemblance to Napoleon, but after this affair we heard no more of this fancied resemblance. General Heth was [now] short, rotund, and square-faced."[9]

None of this cooled support for Heth from R. E. Lee and Jefferson Davis, although a wary Confederate Senate rejected the president's nomination of Heth for rank of major general during the fall of 1862. When the disgruntled brigadier joined the famed Army of Northern Virginia early in 1863, he must have hoped that this new arena would offer a fresh set of opportunities. His arrival cannot have pleased his peers in brigade command in the excellent division commanded by A. P. Hill because Heth outranked all of them, including such seasoned and successful men as J. J. Archer and W. Dorsey Pender. In Hill's absence, the strange newcomer would take command over the able veterans; that circumstance developed during the next battle under difficult conditions.

There is no strong evidence that Heth either embarrassed or distinguished himself when catapulted to division command vice Hill at Chancellorsville. Several of the division's brigades led the way on May 3, but they accomplished what they did without clear indications of the temporary division commander's hand on the helm. Later in the month, with the army turned upside down for reorganization because of Jackson's death, Heth stood in line to take over a division because his rank as brigadier was markedly senior. Since Hill had earned promotion to corps command, his oversized division was an obvious choice for gerrymandering into a new configuration. The six brigades and two others new to the army became two divisions when split in half.

Not surprisingly, Heth's half consisted of the two new brigades (Pettigrew's and Joseph R. Davis's) and the two veteran brigades (Archer's and John M. Brockenbrough's) that had—and still have today—the least distinguished reputations among Hill's original six. Pender's new division would contain Hill's four best brigades, which had fought shoulder-to-shoulder through a spectacularly successful year of victories. Although he must have recognized that it compounded his difficult adjustment, Heth, as the outsider, can hardly have grumbled at this arrangement. Everyone knew that Archer could not serve under Pender, whom he loathed. At Fredericksburg, one of Archer's colonels had been with Pender when a bullet hit the North Carolinian in the hand. After he questioned his colonel about the incident, Archer sputtered nastily, "I wish they had shot him in his damn head." In narrating the incident the colonel added, entirely unnecessarily, "He didn't like him."[10]

As the brand-new division commander advanced his uneven brigades toward Gettysburg on July 1, Archer wound up in the front line just south of the Chambersburg Pike while Davis moved to Archer's left and just north of the pike. Heth's orders were simply "to feel the enemy." As the two brigades pushed across Willoughby Run to open the battle, neither quite knowing where they were going, both of them ran into serious difficulty. Because his field of battle lay south of the road, Archer's disaster falls outside the immediate scope of this study. To summarize Archer's nearby misfortune, he surged forward into an untenable situation without adequate reconnaissance (if any at all) and found Federals in great strength and in advantageous position. One of Archer's Alabamians captured near him expressed the situation vividly when he wrote that suddenly "there were 20,000 Yanks down in among us hollowing surrender." The unfortunate Archer was the first general officer ever taken prisoner from Lee's army. The general and his men stumbled under guard through Gettysburg, a "little town full of red headed women that were bulldozing and cursing us." His captors marched Archer so mercilessly that he "fainted and fell by the roadside." The effects of captivity on the general left him so weak that he died in October 1864 not long after being exchanged to return to Virginia. Although Archer could not have known of the event until long after it occurred, it was the division of his bête noir, Dorsey Pender, that finally swept victorious through the bottom of Willoughby Run that had been so troublesome at the outset of the battle.[11]

Joseph R. Davis led his mixed Mississippi–North Carolina brigade into battle on Archer's left with even less experience to his credit as a division commander than Heth had. His promotion to the rank of brigadier general seems to be as unadulterated an instance of nepotism as the record of the Confederacy offers. Joe Davis's uncle was president of the Confederate States; there seemed little else to commend him (if indeed the relationship deserved commendation). The promotion to brigadier general might be unparalleled in the annals of such things because it shows the tightest imaginable grouping of dates, which usually stretched over many months. Davis was

Brigadier General Joseph Robert Davis.
(Miller's *Photographic History of the Civil War*)

promoted on October 8, 1862, to rank from September 15; won confirmation on the date of promotion, October 8; and accepted on November 1. That unusual sequence probably reflects the political nature of the transaction at a time when the president still had some clout to use. The army found Joe Davis to be "a very unpretending and pleasant gentleman," despite his connections.[12]

No one serving on Joe Davis's staff showed strong signs of having the background, experience, and ability that might help the brigadier meet his responsibilities. The staff member with the most tenure, in fact, suffered from a reputation so bad in both Civil War armies that General Zachary Taylor's grandson (a Federal) thought that "he ought to be kicked out of the Confederacy." Jeb Stuart suggested that the staff officer—thirty-seven-year-old William Thomas Magruder—should have his commission revoked. Stuart encouraged G. W. C. Lee, Jefferson Davis's aide, "to lay this matter before the Prest."[13]

The nine field officers who led the brigade's regiments were similarly bereft of background and skills needed to help Davis cope with the coming battle. Only one of the nine men claimed professional military education or experience before the war (and that one colonel had gone to the U.S. Naval Academy, which of course did not have much to do with infantry training). The three field officers of the 42d Mississippi at Gettysburg, for instance, were a physician, a judge, and a saddler. The colonel commanding the 2d Mississippi admitted after the war to General Davis with refreshing honesty that one of his "most serious difficulties" was that "I almost always lost my bearings."[14]

Davis also came to battle minus one-fourth of his strength because one of his regiments, the 11th Mississippi, had been left behind to guard the division's trains. The 11th would be particularly missed because it was one of two regiments in the brigade with experience in Lee's army. The absence of that unit probably affected the brigade's fate dramatically. The sudden, almost bizarre, turn of events that boxed the brigade in an unusual terrain feature might well have been overcome with a line one-third longer. That raises the question, Why did Heth send forward his weakest brigade as the leading element north of the pike? The answer remains conjectural, but presumably he simply uncoiled the division in the manner it had marched.[15] The order of march traditionally rotated daily, or at least regularly, to spread out the privileges and disadvantages of marching first or eating dust and dodging road debris. Whatever his reasons, if any, Heth made a bad choice when he sent Davis's understrength brigade off to open the battle.

Joe Davis deployed his scant three regiments north of the pike and perpendicular to it—the 2d Mississippi, the 42d Mississippi, and the 55th North Carolina. By this stage of the war, Southern brigades with units from more than one state were decidedly anomalous. By coincidence, Archer's nearby command was the only other mixed brigade out of thirteen in the Third Corps. (The other two infantry corps had just one mixed brigade each.) This Confederate homogeneity by state, which was by no means the rule in the Federal army, was one of Jefferson Davis's organizational fetishes. Finding his handpicked nephew-brigadier in command of one of the very few exceptions to the presidential rule is surprising.

By about 10:30 A.M., General Davis had formed his line of battle on the eastern slopes of Herr Ridge, just west of Willoughby Run. He put his North Carolinians on the left, with their left extended about twelve hundred feet north of the pike. The 2d Mississippi formed battle line to the right of the 55th North Carolina, and the 42d Mississippi prepared to advance on the brigade right, with its flank right on the pike.[16] Perhaps Davis positioned the 2d Mississippi in the middle to provide a leavening of experience to the new regiments on either side. The 2d and the unfortunately absent 11th had served with distinction in Evander M. Law's brigade before they fell victim to the shuffling demanded by Joe Davis's uncle in the interest of tidy tables of organization. The 2d had spent the entire preceding night on picket so the men can hardly have been fresh and ready.[17] Poor Davis deserved the chance to start this day in reserve, but Heth directed otherwise.

The 55th North Carolina began the advance with its left touching the run, so it faced the chore of getting through the

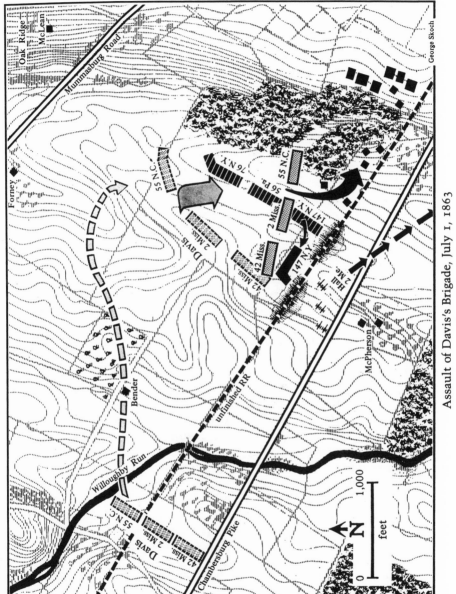

Assault of Davis's Brigade, July 1, 1863

George Skoch

wet bottom almost at once. The two Mississippi regiments soon crossed too, though the course of the run put it farther to their front. Their comrades under Archer across the pike had found the run thick with both nettles and armed foemen, but if Davis's men experienced any difficulty none of them reported it. Almost at once the 55th began to swing out leftward in an arc that took it farther north as well as east, past the Bender house and into the adjacent orchard. The left of the 2d Mississippi also stretched into the edge of the orchard. After the war the colonel commanding the 55th returned to the field and showed the battlefield's leading contemporary historian, John B. Bachelder, exactly where his regiment had passed through the northeast corner of Bender's orchard. Emmor B. Cope, a surveyor and mapper who became famous for his work at both Gettysburg and Sharpsburg, marked the spot, which proved to be fully two thousand feet from the pike.[18] The leftward drift of the 55th would turn out to be tactically advantageous, but loosening the line by eight hundred feet during a short advance gave evidence of some uncertainty, and two thousand feet was an extremely broad front for three regiments to cover.

Because of the nature of the ground and its leftward loop, the 55th North Carolina drew the first fire from the Federals, who were themselves newly arrived on the field. The initial round struck two men of the 55th's color guard, as though in forecast of a day in which the men around the colors would suffer even more heavily than was customary. The 2d Mississippi, to the 55th's right, could see the Federal line at the far edge of the broad field of wheat. "They were in the wheat . . . lying down, though plainly seen," one of the Mississippians wrote, "while their officers rode up and down their lines." The 42d, down next to the pike, reached the diagonal path of the run after the other two regiments. "The enemy's skirmish line was posted along this brooklet, and we soon began to hear the peculiar hiss of the minnie ball," a soldier of the 42d recalled.[19] The advancing Confederates, all under fire and with their target in view, gathered momentum as they swept through the wheat on their broad front.

The distance from Davis's line of departure to the hurriedly formed Federal line measured about one thousand yards. The Federals preparing to receive them included three regiments, from north to south the 76th New York, 56th Pennsylvania, and 147th New York. Given the pronounced advantage of the defensive and the inexperience of most of the Confederates, three Federal regiments ought to have been able to repulse three attacking regiments without inordinate strain. In the event, however, Davis's brigade swept its foe off the ridge and won what seemed for a time to be a crucial victory to open the fighting in that sector.

Davis's surprising initial success was by no means easily achieved. The 2d Mississippi moved steadily "up the slope to within good shot of their line," when the Federals "jumped to their feet" out of the wheat and opened fire. The 42d "advanced steadily and rapidly up the hill" but only by braving a fire that rapidly sent two score of its men back with wounds to a forward hospital set up under some trees near Willoughby Run. The stalwart advance of those two regiments could hardly have produced any positive results, however, without the 55th North Carolina's fortunate positioning on the far left. As the regimental historian noted: "The left of our regiment extended considerably beyond the right of the enemy's line— and at the proper time our left was wheeled to the right. The enemy fled from the field with great loss."[20] The extended left of the 55th, a circumstance more than likely coincidental rather than designed, decided the result of the engagement.

The color guard of the 55th, which had suffered the loss of first blood at long range, drew more fire as it closed with the 76th New York. The sergeant carrying the flag went down about one hundred yards from the New Yorkers' line and Colonel John Kerr Connally grabbed the falling flag. Connally—the erstwhile Naval Academy sailor—had provoked General W. Dorsey Pender's unequivocal wrath earlier in the war, prompting the North Carolina general to call the colonel "very ridiculous . . . a most conceited fellow." On this July morning, Colonel Connally performed under fire up to any standard that Pender or anyone else could desire. As he waved aloft his unit's flag and wheeled it around to the right in the pivotal tactical maneuver, the colonel fell severely wounded in two places. Major Alfred H. Belo rushed over to the fallen regimental commander and asked anxiously if Connally was badly wounded. "Yes," the colonel answered through his pain, "but do not pay any attention to me; take the colors and keep ahead of the Mississippians." Connally fell 315 feet from where the 76th New York monument now stands, at a point in the southwestern corner of the modern battlefield tour road.[21]

Although the 55th's sweeping wheel determined the result, keeping ahead of the Mississippians would take some doing. Lieutenant A. K. Roberts of the 2d led a dash forward near the seam between the two Mississippi regiments that broke into the 56th Pennsylvania's front and captured a flag, at the cost of the lieutenant's life. As the Federal line came unhinged and streamed away to its left rear, the Mississippians swarmed into their midst and took about three hundred prisoners. The 42d, from its position closest to the focus of the retreat, netted the largest haul. Some men of the 2d thought they saw cavalry in the woods behind the Northern position and fired a volley that knocked down several men and horses; they later decided that they had fired on mounted officers and their staff members.[22]

The Confederate success and the Federal collapse did not unfold evenly, of course. Knots of Federals continued to make what Davis called "a stubborn resistance," and a substantial number (mainly of the 147th New York) rallied on the Confederate right near an unfinished railroad that soon would bring grief to the Southerners. Northern gunners of Hall's 2d Maine Battery, firing from just beyond the railroad line, contributed valiantly to the efforts to delay Davis's victorious troops. Some Federal infantry also mustered a brief threat to what was now the left rear of the Confederate line, after it had swung toward the railroad.[23]

Even as Davis and his regiments were enjoying the delirium of a sweeping and well-earned victory, the instruments of their destruction were gathering in a random grouping just across the pike. The 6th Wisconsin of the famed Iron Brigade had angled northwestward toward the pike, diverging from its sister regiments as they headed approximately due west well south of the pike. The two northernmost regiments (84th and 95th New York) of the force that had been facing Archer also began to move toward what obviously was a threatened point. The two New York regiments had not been much involved in Archer's easy repulse; had the Southern attack south of the pike been better managed, the 84th and 95th would not have had the leisure to figure in Davis's sector.

The completion of the Confederate reorientation through ninety degrees, from an advance due east to a facing of due south, came about according to one North Carolinian in response to the sight of the Wisconsin regiment moving across the fields toward the pike. The 147th New York viewed the Wisconsin men as their saviors, which confirms the close timing. Many other Southerners probably faced toward the Maine battery position. While some of the Mississippians and Carolinians had advanced beyond the railroad and others had not, that commanding feature soon lured them like a malignant magnet into its deceptively protective shelter. Joe Davis had neither the experience nor the grasp to recognize this deadfall for what it was. Colonel John M. Stone, commanding the 2d Mississippi, wrote to Davis after the war about the events of this day and included with unconscious irony one of the general's favorite stories about the difficulty of achieving a large perspective in battle: "General, I was very much like the French Soldier of whom you sometimes told us, who never saw anything while the battle was going on except the rump of his fat file leader. In battle I rarely knew anything that occured beyond the immediate vicinity of my own command." That honest admission of a universal combat truth doubtless applied to the original storyteller, Joe Davis, in the chaotic moments when his men clustered in a deep cut of the railroad line, binding themselves up in sheaves for delivery to Northern prison camps.[24]

The railroad line ran through the countryside west of Gettysburg on a mixture of grades and cuts resulting from the usual engineering efforts to flatten the route. As was the case with several other unfinished lines made famous by the Civil

War (at Second Manassas, Chancellorsville, and the Wilderness, for instance), the nascent railroad industry had accomplished much of its work but had not quite gotten into operation when the war interrupted such civilian endeavor. The unfinished line west of Gettysburg, in the words of a Carolinian under Davis, "had been graded but not ironed." A very deep and steeply walled cut that proved Davis's undoing was not very long, west to east, and could have been readily avoided with a modicum of intelligent leadership. As the Confederates flocked into the cut, the 42d Mississippi on the right and some of the 2d Mississippi found its illusory deep shelter. The color guard of the 2d, though, was far enough east that "the ditch was not more than two feet deep" and thus formed ideal shelter without restricting movement or firing positions. The entire 55th North Carolina on the left (east) of the position was free from the hampering aspect of the deep cut. A carefully surveyed stake placed after the war at the eastern end of the Carolinians' line was 109 yards from the center of the bridge over the cut.[25]

The three Southern regiments at the railroad line suffered from the disorganization inherent in victory nearly as much as in defeat. They had covered a long distance under fire and stress and were, Davis reported, "all much exhausted by the excessive heat." An alarming number of their regimental leaders had gone down wounded or killed. Seven of the nine field officers would be casualties by noon. Although it is impossible to time each of those losses, many of them had fallen before the crisis at the railroad. The 55th, for instance, had already lost not only Colonel Connally opposite the 76th New York but also its lieutenant colonel, Maurice Thompson Smith. Smith, a thirty-five-year-old planter educated at Chapel Hill, suffered a mortal wound while beyond the railroad. The commander of the 2d Mississippi had been shot off the top rail of a fence as he climbed over.[26] Disorganization spawned by movement and victory, by exhaustion, and by loss of command and control through regimental leadership all contributed to the disaster stalking Davis, but none of them mattered as much as the dreadful limitations of the railroad cut position.

The Federals opposite Davis—especially the 6th Wisconsin and its stalwart commander, Lieutenant Colonel Rufus R. Dawes—soon launched an attack, the valor of which made possible a victory that reaped the opportunities presented by the railroad cut. Three Northern regiments faced two hundred yards of naked turf, interrupted only by fences that help up men climbing over them as slow-moving targets. From west to east the Federal attackers included the 84th New York, the 95th New York, and the 6th Wisconsin. From west to east the Confederates faced them with the 42d Mississippi, 2d Mississippi, and 55th North Carolina. The alignment was not as crisp as that enumeration suggests, of course.

As Dawes pushed his men through swarms of bullets toward the railroad, the two New York regiments closed on his left and somewhat behind him. The appearance of a nicely coordinated attack was misleading; cooperation was all but accidental at the outset. One of Dawes's aides had the good idea of sending a fifty-man detachment out to the east to close that route of escape from the cut to the Confederates and put his notion into operation without any delay during the attack across the deadly field.[27]

The Northerners lost heavily in the attack, but a considerable part of the line that they approached was all but silent because the deep part of the cut left its defenders unable to see out and fire at their assailants. Much later that day another Confederate brigade occupied the same line (in enough strength to stretch wide beyond the cut so it came to no grief), and one of its men described vividly the difficulties of firing from the deep point toward the field and its fences:

> Taking up a musket, I managed with difficulty to crawl to the top of the embankment, and saw the enemy drawn up in line . . . behind an old Virginia worm fence. They soon began to advance, but with no alacrity for the work. Seeing a field officer in front, urging them on whilst waving his hat, the thought occurred that his loss might be of considerable advantage to us in checking the advance. He fell on the instant . . . and letting myself aloose at the top, [I only] recovered an upright position at

Repulse of Davis's Brigade, July 1, 1863

Bender

Willoughby Run

unfinished RR

Chambersburg Pike

McPherson

Davis

42 Miss.

2 Miss.

55 N.C.

84 N.Y.

95 N.Y.

6 Wis.

Cutler

N

0   1,000

feet

George Skoch

the bottom, but in a dilapidated plight. A jutting root or jagged rock caught in my breeches' leg and tore it from the bottom, to the top, losing [my] hat also in the fall.[28]

Enough Southern muskets east of the cut could bear on the Wisconsin men to hit them hard, but they crossed the interval in the face of their losses and struck the Confederates in a brief flurry of hand-to-hand fighting. G. W. Bynum of the 2d Mississippi "was so close on the enemy when wounded that the paper attached to the . . . cartridge was forced into his leg." The color guard of that regiment "were all killed and wounded in less than five minutes"; more than a dozen bullets perforated their flag, and the staff was hit and splintered two or three times. A squad of blue-clad enemies closed on the Mississippi colors, but a volley knocked them all down. More came behind them. A lieutenant reaching for the trophy collapsed with a bullet in the shoulder. One Mississippian killed a Wisconsin soldier, then fell to a rifle butt wielded by another attacker. After a dozen Northerners had been shot down, a large soldier gathered up both the flag and its last defender, who had torn the colors from the splintered staff.[29]

Federals coming up opposite the 55th North Carolina saw Major Alfred H. Belo—a particularly feisty officer who fought a famous wartime duel against the Confederate Englishman John Cussons—and identified him as the soul of the defense in that sector. A Federal officer hurled his sword like a javelin at Belo, missing the major but striking a man behind him. The swordless Northerner shouted, "Kill that officer, and that will end it," but Confederate rifles silenced him instead.[30] Farther west, where the cut was a deep deathtrap, the attackers quickly ended the fighting when they lined the southern lip of the chasm and pointed their weapons down into it. The blocking force of Northerners sent to the east end of the cut added to the scope of the Confederate disaster, although apparently this cork in Davis's bottle slipped into place west of most of the North Carolinians, who streamed north unhampered by the level railroad grade there.

Davis had lost perhaps 600 men, and the Federal forces that faced him in both halves of his battle lost about 850. The first phase of the fight north of the pike had produced a striking success for Davis that turned quickly into a bitter disaster. As an extended lull settled on the field, masses of Federal prisoners moved westward and about the same number of Confederate prisoners were herded eastward. One unwounded Mississippian seethed for the rest of his life about his treatment as a prisoner. One of the guards "punched me in the side," he grumbled, and made the luckless Confederate give up "the finest field glasses that I ever saw." Thirty-seven years later on the anniversary of the battle the robbed prisoner still cherished a fantasy: "I would like very much to meet up with him now." A wounded Confederate who remained on the field until July 5 had better luck with his captors. Within thirty minutes after Lee's rear guard passed, Union cavalry came past the railroad cut with the task of smashing abandoned Confederate weapons. A Federal picked up a rifle next to the wounded man by its muzzle, raised it high over his head, and smashed it on a nearby rock. The concussion fired the weapon by some freak, and the bullet dropped the Northerner dead on the ground, leaving the wounded prisoner to yearn, "O for a thousand such guns!"[31]

The railroad cut saw more fighting later on July 1, hours after Davis's collapse. Confederates would occupy it and then sweep through the area in triumph. Federals used the railroad line as a corridor of retreat when the day went against them. One of Davis's men watched artillery falling on the retreating foe and thought that "every shell seemed to bring down a dozen men." A North Carolinian who saw the same retreat from the vicinity of the cut thought the Confederate artillery firing down the railroad line was so horribly effective that he "could almost hear their bones crunch under the shot and shell." A Virginian marching down the railroad toward town that evening with Edward Johnson's division—the last military use of the now-famous unfinished railroad—was shocked by the "gruesome sights in the railroad cut," where bodies were torn apart to a degree astonishing even to a veteran.[32]

When Davis's brigade scattered in various directions just after noon on July 1, perhaps the more thoughtful of its leaders began asking the questions that persist to this day. No doubt in the painful aftermath of their ordeal they would have been more inclined to grimace than to smile sadly over the unintentional drollery of General Heth's official summary of the joint disasters that befell Davis and Archer. "The enemy had now been felt," Heth wrote with accidental irony, "and found to be in heavy force in and around Gettysburg."[33]

Several questions that Heth did not address, and that we still cannot answer, stand out starkly under what we must admit is the somewhat unfairly pitiless glare of hindsight. Why was Pender's strong and all-veteran division not at the front for this delicate operation, rather than Heth's weak and largely untested force? If Heth must take the point, why put Davis in the front line instead of Pettigrew's larger brigade, or even Brockenbrough's? It is difficult to imagine the fiasco at the railroad cut developing against a four-regiment front, such as a normal brigade would show: the deadly deep spot in the cut is not that extensive. A line one-third longer than Davis's likely would have lacerated the flanks of the Wisconsin and New York attackers unbearably from the railroad and perhaps even advanced on one flank or the other to make the Federal position entirely untenable.

Where were the Southern division and corps commanders who might have been expected to superintend green commanders and green troops at a critical moment? Heth was far enough to the rear that he had no impact whatsoever on Davis's defeat, and A. P. Hill was nearly ten miles away at Cashtown, totally insulated from the action. By contrast, Hill's Union counterpart, John F. Reynolds, hurried to the front, where he was able to inspirit the defense and throw troops into the decisive zone. Reynolds paid with his life for being in the thick of things, but not before he had done his job successfully. Hill did not do his job at all, and Heth did not do his competently.

After the wrong Confederate troops went into action, without adequate high-level supervision, events raised a surprising new tactical question: Why did three Confederate regiments succeed in a direct attack against three Federal regiments, despite the advantages of the defensive, then succumb—while on the defensive—to an attack by three more Federal regiments? Conventional wisdom would suggest that the defenders would win in both instances and could hardly countenance a complete double reversal of form. Two obvious circumstances help to explain Davis's reverse while defending the cut: the abysmal position where the cut deepened and the cumulative effect of two battles, the second against a fresh set of foes. Two other factors also deserve consideration: good colonels and the advantages of the offensive side in choosing its ground and exploiting momentum. Colonels Connally and Dawes played important roles from opposite sides of the line in Davis's initial success and in his eventual disaster. Removing Connally from the 55th North Carolina and introducing Dawes into the scene at the railroad cut helped tip the scales. Both successful attacking forces had the freedom of the aggressor to choose the setting at the moment of decision, and each did so to good effect. The 55th swung left to make the position of the 76th New York and its companions untenable, and the Federals later corked the end of the railroad cut to good effect. Both successful attackers then sealed their triumph by exploiting momentum that turned into victories greater than the sum of their parts would have suggested.

For an hour after Davis's collapse, the battlefield north of the Chambersburg Pike lay quiet under the midday sun. Then, from the north, Confederates from Richard S. Ewell's Second Corps began to filter into the area. They were the advanced guard of Robert E. Rodes's division, and they represented a stroke of good fortune that would win July 1 for the Army of Northern Virginia. While Federals facing west had soundly rebuffed Heth, Rodes was moving toward their rear on an axis perpendicular to the Federal line of fire. The fortuitous arrival of Rodes and the rest of Ewell's force behind him doomed the Federal position where Archer and Davis had come to grief, despite two further Confederate disasters on the new front some thousand yards northeast of the railroad cut.

Ewell's Second Corps of the Army of Northern Virginia had been brilliantly successful on many fields under the leadership of the late lamented Stonewall Jackson. Although the new corps commander had missed nine extremely active months of the army's history, his return to command had seemed brightly auspicious during the movement north. Ewell had thrashed Federals under Robert H. Milroy at Winchester about as well as Jackson ever had done, and in Stonewall's own Shenandoah Valley, too. On the morning of July 1, Ewell rode with Rodes's division as it moved south toward Gettysburg. The troops that followed them exhibited an élan forged from good leadership and an unbroken string of successes. An experienced Second Corps officer wrote: "One thing is certain: Lee's army was never in better spirits or morale than it exhibited at Gettysburg. It never seemed to me as invincible as on the 1st July 1863."[34]

Robert E. Rodes advanced toward the open flank of the Federal First Corps at Gettysburg facing not only a golden tactical opportunity but also his first battle as a major general commanding a division. At Chancellorsville, Rodes had commanded the same division (it had been D. H. Hill's for the preceding year) as its ranking brigadier general, and with marked success. Now it belonged to him permanently.

Rodes would craft a fine record at the division's head during the fourteen months of life left to him. In fact, he stands among the best division commanders—I think the very best—in an army full of famous units and famous men. Not least among his talents was the ability to inspire subordinates. Young James Power Smith of Jackson's staff wrote of Rodes early in 1863: "I like him so much. He is very much admired by all and very popular." Perhaps his appeal grew in part from a striking martial appearance; a member of Jeb Stuart's staff called Rodes and Pender "the most splendid looking soldiers of the war." Another element of Rodes's popularity was based on a bluff personality featuring "blunt speech" and a tincture of "blarney." The new major general's wry style shone through an episode from the winter after Gettysburg, when corps commander Ewell was steadily succumbing to a combination of physical and domestic ailments. Rodes "laughingly" asked a visiting chaplain, "Who commanded the Second Corps, whether Mrs. Ewell, General Ewell, or Sandy Pendleton, hoping it was the last."[35]

Major General Robert Emmett Rodes.
(Miller's *Photographic History of the Civil War*)

On July 1, 1863, Ewell's decline was not yet obvious and Rodes's rise in esteem had only just begun. The pivotal individuals in the opening round of the division's fight on Oak Ridge were of lower rank, however, and Rodes had the misfortune to be ill-served by both brigade commanders who led—or were supposed to lead—the forward units. Junius Daniel, S. Dodson Ramseur, and George Doles fought superbly at the head of Rodes's brigades at Gettysburg and would do so on many future fields; but Alfred Iverson and Edward A. O'Neal opened the July 1 fight for Rodes in execrable fashion.

As Rodes drew near the booming guns west of Gettysburg, he discovered in Oak Ridge a convenient ally: "I found that by keeping along the wooded ridge, on the left side of which the town of Gettysburg is situated, I could strike the force of the enemy with which General Hill's troops were engaged upon the flank, and that, besides moving under cover, whenever we struck the enemy we could engage him with the advantage in ground." The situation seemed ideal. Rodes was pointed squarely at a vulnerable Federal point, he had a wooded ridge to cover his approach, and the height of his protecting ridge assured him of a commanding position whenever he established hostile contact. Rodes initially advanced south down Oak Ridge on a narrow front just one brigade wide, but as the ground permitted he widened the front until it included, from right to left, Iverson, O'Neal, and Doles. All of this wheeling and re-aligning imposed added exertion on the troops, especially in those regiments serving as outriders for the wheels. The 5th Alabama, for instance, covered the last one and one-half miles at an uncomfortable pace—"frequently at a run"—across "very rough" ground that included mature wheat fields, freshly plowed ground, orchards, gardens, and wood and stone fences. The regimental commander reported that the ordeal fatigued every soldier and caused "many of them to faint from exhaustion."[36]

As the Confederates reached the edge of the woods north of the Forney farm, a vista south and west of them unfolded as though on a massive relief map. The coup d'oeil so often sought (and so rarely found) on confusing Civil War battlefields took away the breath of officers and soldiers alike. A member of the 6th Alabama wrote that they could plainly see A. P. Hill's troops "away to our right across broad fields of ripe wheat . . . moving slowly but steadily on the long blue lines." This novel vantage point "was the only time during the war that we were in position to get such a view of contending forces. It seemed like some grand panorama with the sounds of conflict added." Rodes, with the responsibility for exploiting the chance in mind, reported that "the whole of that portion of the force opposing General Hill's troops could be seen."[37]

Rodes at once ordered his supporting artillery up to occupy the commanding knob that overlooked the Forney farm and the fields sloping toward the railroad and the Chambersburg Pike just beyond it. The division's outstanding artillery chief, Lieutenant Colonel Thomas Hill Carter, sent his own old battery, the King William Artillery, together with Captain Charles W. Fry's Orange Artillery, to open on the enemy below the knob and "to enfilade the enemy's lines and batteries." The time by now was about 1:00 P.M. Less than an hour had passed since the curtain fell on Davis's disaster at the railroad cut.[38]

Carter's fire hurt the Federals opposite him, but it also brought down on his position a storm of counter-battery fire. The colonel reported that his two batteries "fired with very decided effect, compelling the infantry to take shelter in the railroad cut"—that cut so deadly a trap in the face of infantry attack but so wonderfully useful for protection against artillery rounds. For its good shooting, the King William company paid with a dozen casualties, or about 20 percent of its engaged strength. Shells exploding "fiercely" among the men of the Alabama brigade took their toll. One killed a captain in the 12th Alabama while that regiment waited in the woods; another badly wounded two men. Colonel O'Neal styled the artillery exchange "a severe engagement" and estimated its duration as a full hour. Colonel Samuel Bonneau Pickens of the 12th (a Citadel graduate still a few days short of his twenty-fourth birthday) echoed O'Neal on both the severity and duration of

The Town of Gettysburg from Oak Hill.
(Battles and Leaders of the Civil War)

the artillery affair. Rodes eventually ordered his Alabamians back into the woods for better shelter from Northern shells.[39]

As Rodes prepared to send his troops into battle, covering his activity with Carter's artillery fire, the vacuum in front of him began to turn into a more substantial, if still chaotic, Federal presence. The Union Eleventh Corps began to come onto the field to Rodes's left by 1:00 P.M., and the two brigades of General John C. Robinson's First Corps division took up positions on the Forney farm right in front of the Confederates. The brigades of Generals Gabriel R. Paul and Henry Baxter hurried into line behind stone and wood fences approximately at right angles to Rodes's proper line of advance. Their awkward location should have made Paul and Baxter ready targets for Rodes, but they would inflict grievous losses from their flawed position on maladroitly led Southern brigades under O'Neal and Iverson.

From his elevated post of observation Rodes could see what seemed to be enemy units closing in on him: "The enemy began to show large bodies of men in front of the town, most of which were directed upon the position which I held, and almost at the same time a portion of the force opposed to General Hill changed position so as to occupy the woods on the summit of the same ridge I occupied . . . directly opposite my center." The troops to his left—the Eleventh Corps—Rodes would hold at bay by the expedient of putting George Doles's sturdy Georgia brigade out in that direction, even though it meant that a gap would exist between Doles's right and O'Neal's left. That should suffice "until General Early's division arrived," Rodes thought, which he knew would happen soon and to good effect.[40]

That left O'Neal to advance southward down the steep eastern slopes of the ridge, in tandem with Iverson's parallel move down the crest of the ridge. Daniel's big but new brigade would advance en echelon behind Iverson's right. Ramseur's excellent regiments would be in close reserve to exploit the first opportunity.

This straightforward and eminently workable plan ran afoul of poor reconnaissance, which was Rodes's fault (recognition of the precise Federal alignment would have suggested weighting his left more heavily); it stumbled upon sturdy Federal resistance; but more than anything else the advance foundered on the nicely matched incompetence of O'Neal and Iverson. O'Neal's advance began somewhat before Iverson's—therein lay some of the tale—and it led directly to Iverson's difficulty so it requires the initial review.

Edward Asbury O'Neal was an Alabama lawyer who dabbled in politics, not always successfully before the war, though he became governor after the war. He was forty-four years old at Gettysburg. Nothing O'Neal had studied or experienced before 1861 had prepared him for military command at any level. He was an ardent secessionist and extraordinarily well connected with powerful leaders. On that basis O'Neal won early rank, which put him in position for advancement by seniority later in the war.

Rodes apparently maintained cordial relations with O'Neal (Edward A. O'Neal, Jr., served Rodes as a volunteer aide-de-camp at Chancellorsville and Gettysburg), but the division commander did not think that his subordinate had the potential for advancement. Although O'Neal was senior colonel in his brigade, Rodes formally recommended another officer for

Colonel Edward Asbury O'Neal.
(Miller's *Photographic History of the Civil War*)

promotion in a letter to the corps commander in mid-May 1863. Rodes mentioned O'Neal but clearly did not want him promoted. Neither of the two colonels whom Rodes did want—John B. Gordon and John T. Morgan, both of whom became general officers in due course—was known to R. E. Lee, nor was O'Neal. Complications also intervened with the other two so Lee suggested that seniority should be followed. O'Neal, wrote Lee to Jefferson Davis, "has been identified with his regiment and the brigade by long service as Lieut. Col. and Colonel."[41] Richmond accordingly forwarded to the army a commission as brigadier general for O'Neal, dated June 6, 1863.

Immediately after Gettysburg the army high command began taking steps to ensure an arrangement that would keep O'Neal from both brigade command and general's rank. Lee returned O'Neal's commission to Richmond and had it canceled, but for most of the rest of the war the issue continued to haunt the army commander, to his considerable disgust. Three weeks after Gettysburg most of the officers of the Alabama brigade signed a circular letter to Jefferson Davis lauding O'Neal's valor and expressing appreciation for the way he had treated them. Perhaps significantly, the letter did not tout O'Neal's skill noticeably. Cullen A. Battle, who would be O'Neal's eventual replacement, signed first. This letter was framed under the impression that O'Neal would be leaving the Army of Northern Virginia immediately. On August 1, Rodes wrote to Lee through Walter H. Taylor, reiterating his opposition to having O'Neal in high authority. Having given up on getting Gordon or Morgan, Rodes now endorsed Battle with the earnest hope that "his appointment . . . will be made promptly, because until the Brigade has a permanent commander, and a better one in a disciplinary character than it has had lately it is likely to continue in a condition that is not at all satisfactory to any one concerned."[42]

Colonel O'Neal expended considerable energy and vast pools of ink in pressing his claim that his commission as brigadier general was withdrawn illegally. He mustered in support a mighty array of political correspondence. The governor of

Alabama wrote repeatedly to Jefferson Davis in that vein. Letters signed by dozens of state legislators reached the War Department attesting to such of O'Neal's virtues as being the best orator in Alabama and owning a striking appearance. The net volume of political material in O'Neal's records (and typically not all of such manuscripts survive) is at least twice as extensive as the logrolling political paperwork in any other Confederate service record I have ever seen.[43]

In the spring of 1864, as Lee prepared for a death struggle with Grant, he still faced grumbling from O'Neal and his political friends. The commanding general wrote to Jefferson Davis that O'Neal's complaint "has been presented to me several times" but that the accession to command of Rodes's old brigade had been made on the basis of pressing "military considerations." Lee's usually calm style showed some hairline cracks when he wrote: "I feel aggrieved at this repeated charge of injustice, & but that we are upon the eve of a campaign . . . I should ask for a court of Inquiry into the matter." A few weeks later O'Neal marshaled a new argument in his struggle for promotion when he forwarded the novel notion that his salary as colonel was inadequate for his family's financial needs and he therefore must have a general's pay. Whether or not Lee saw that letter, there is no record of any comment, but he doubtless would have joined most others who read it in marveling at the precedent proposed by a man who outranked all but a few score of the hundreds of thousands of individuals in Confederate service. Two weeks after O'Neal wrote his low-salary letter, Lee washed his hands of the matter with finality. The army commander wrote bluntly that he had lately "made more particular inquiries into his capacity to command the brigade and I cannot recommend him to the command." O'Neal remained a colonel.[44]

What O'Neal did at Gettysburg on July 1 that led to cancellation of his commission was to lose control of his brigade at a crucial moment; perhaps he never had control from the beginning. He compounded this felony by failing to lead—or even to follow—his troops in their important attack. O'Neal put a finishing touch on his performance by grumbling in his official report weeks after the battle that he had not figured out what happened to his various regiments, even though the reports of his subordinates showed that they had grasped events with easy clarity.

The attack of O'Neal's brigade down the eastern slope of Oak Ridge toward the Mummasburg Road included only three of its five regiments. The reduction in numbers and the resultant reduction in width of the brigade front drastically hampered the attack. Rodes himself pulled one of the regiments— the 5th Alabama—out of line and sent it down the ridge behind the rest of the brigade as a makeshift measure to protect the yawning gap that stretched eastward to Doles's right. The 3d Alabama failed to advance with its mates because of O'Neal's disorientation. That came about when Rodes pushed the brigade back into the woods for protection during the artillery duel. He carefully aligned the 3d Alabama (on O'Neal's far right) with Daniel's left unit (the Second North Carolina Battalion), to be sure that his weak brigade commander knew what to do, then ordered O'Neal to use that as his point of reference for the rest of the Alabama regiments. When the temporary expedient for dodging artillery ended, O'Neal evidently concluded that since Rodes had placed the 3d once, it no longer was his own to direct. No one told Daniel that the orphaned 3d Alabama was his to run because no one but O'Neal had that in mind. The colonel of the regiment tried to stay aligned with Daniel, but the North Carolinian reasonably enough responded to a request for instructions with word that the Alabama regiment should operate independently.[45]

The 3d Alabama felt its forlorn lot keenly. An officer in the regiment wrote that Daniel "said he did not have room for us. All this time firing going on and we losing men could not leave the field and had nothing to fight." Although the official reports by officers of both the 3d and the 5th (two for the latter) were written soon after the battle and reported clearly on the circumstances affecting the regiments on July 1, O'Neal's report, written on July 24, insisted querulously: "Why my brigade was thus deprived of two regiments, I have never been informed."[46]

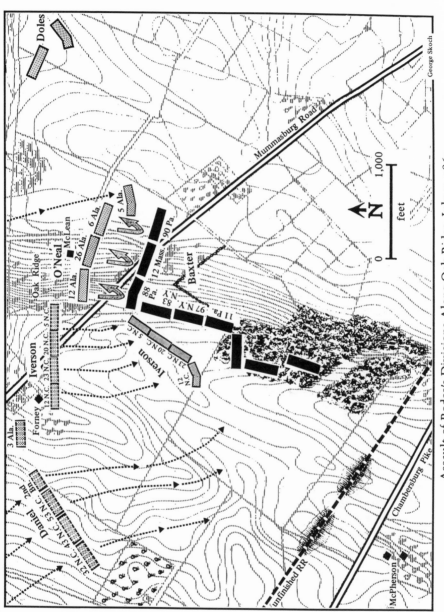

Assault of Rodes's Divisions Along Oak Ridge, July 1, 1863

George Skoch

Doles

Oak Ridge

O'Neal

12 Ala.   26 Ala.   6 Ala.   5 Ala.

McLean

90 Pa.

12 Mass.

Baxter

88 Pa.

97 N.Y.

83 N.Y.

11 Pa.

Iverson

Forney

3 Ala.

12 N.C.   23 N.C.   20 N.C.   5 N.C.

Iverson

12 N.C.   23 N.C.   20 N.C.

Mummasburg Road

N

1,000

feet

0

Daniel

2d Brig.

2 N.C.   43 N.C.   45 N.C.   53 N.C.

unfinished RR

Chambersburg Pike

McPherson

At about 2:15 P.M., Rodes, cognizant of O'Neal's need for special attention, gave the Alabama lawyer the order to attack and indicated to him "precisely the point to which he was to direct the left of the four regiments then under his orders." At that tense moment, O'Neal announced that for some reason (none is of record, and it is hard to imagine a persuasive excuse) he and his entire staff were without horses. The subject came up when Rodes discovered that the 3d Alabama was missing because of O'Neal's confusion, and it became necessary for Rodes to send a lieutenant of his own staff far to the right in what proved to be a vain attempt to attach the lost regiment to Daniel's brigade.[47]

Even the pared-down three-regiment Alabama attack might have met with success had it been properly coordinated with Iverson's advance and, equally important, had it moved far enough east to enfilade the Federal position. As Rodes reported disgustedly: "The three . . . regiments moved with alacrity (but not in accordance with my orders as to direction) and in confusion into the action." The Union commanders whose soldiers had been faced nominally westward had recognized the vulnerability of their right flank and rear along the Mummasburg Road and swung regiments out to provide some protection. The resulting line came to be known from its shape as the Hook. One of the regiments in the refused portion of the line was the 12th Massachusetts. Its adjutant remembered that the Alabama troops relished the protection of the big red barn of the McLean farm. From "behind this, and under its cover the enemy . . . deployed in several columns to the right (our left) we firing upon them as best we could."[48] Fortunately for the 12th Massachusetts and its companions in arms, the Alabama troops were moving away from the Federal weakness and into the Federal strength.

Given the misdirection of the feeble attack, its repulse by the Federals is hardly surprising. A member of the 88th Pennsylvania positioned near the Hook reported the easy victory almost nonchalantly: "Their line of battle, covered by a cloud of busy skirmishers, came driving through the woods from the right of the Mummasburg Road. Waiting until they were in easy range, the order was given, 'Commence firing.' With the sharp crack of the muskets a fleecy cloud of smoke rolled down the front of the brigade and the Minie balls zipped and buzzed with a merry chorus toward the Southern line, which halted, and after a brief contest, retired to the shelter of the woods."[49]

The view from the other end of the firing range was, of course, far less comfortable. Rodes wrote, "It was soon apparent that we were making no impression upon the enemy." Colonel Pickens of the 12th Alabama thought that the "desperate fight" lasted only "about fifteen minutes." Robert E. Park of that regiment lay down flat and urged his men to keep cool and continue firing while he tended to wounded comrades. "Balls were falling thick and fast around us, and whizzing past and often striking some one near." A round finally hit Park in the hip. He later recalled, "It was a wonder, a miracle, I was not afterward shot a half dozen times." Not surprisingly, Park thought his ordeal consisted of "long exposure" rather than just fifteen minutes. Through the whole frightful episode, Major Adolph Proskauer of the 12th inspired everyone within visual range. The twenty-four-year-old German-born officer was the "best dressed man in the regiment . . . very handsome" and clearly very brave too. The wounded Park marveled at how "our gallant Jew Major smoked his cigars calmly and coolly in the thickest of the fight."[50]

While Major Proskauer waxed calm at the eye of the storm, General Rodes discovered to his astonishment that O'Neal had not accompanied his troops into action. When the plight of the three misdirected Alabama regiments became apparent to him, Rodes hurried back to the 5th Alabama, guarding the gap in the direction of Doles's brigade, intending to use the regiment in this emergency. Rodes reported officially, with a mixture of restraint and blunt apportionment of blame: "To my surprise, in giving this command to its colonel (Hall), I found that Colonel O'Neal, instead of personally superintending the movements of his brigade, had chosen to remain with his reserve regiment. The result was that the whole brigade . . . was repulsed quickly, and with loss."[51]

The 5th Alabama did move forward in an attempt to ease the plight of its three sister regiments. The sharpshooter battalion of the brigade, commanded by the major of the 5th, served as a gauzy screen providing tenuous linkage between O'Neal's shivered left and the right of Doles while the main body of the 5th moved south. The 5th formed an obtuse angle for a time, part of the regiment facing east and part of it south toward O'Neal's difficulties. When the main body of the brigade fell back, the 5th returned to its starting point and resumed its original mission guarding the chasm between the ridge and Doles. The 5th received an invaluable boost in both of its roles—guarding the gap toward Doles and assisting its stricken comrades—from fire poured out by the Virginia artillery battery commanded by Captain R. C. M. Page. The Virginians went into position at the eastern foot of the ridge behind the McLean farm, at a considerable elevation disadvantage, and hurled shells into the Federals facing O'Neal as well as southeastward toward enemy units opposite the gap. Page lost the enormous total, for a single battery, of thirty casualties, and he lost seventeen horses as well.[52]

The break in O'Neal's front began, predictably, at his misplaced left flank. The regiment there, the 6th Alabama, should have been farther east beyond the Federal point at the Hook according to Rodes's design and in keeping with every tactical rule. The collapse of the 6th spread steadily westward. All of the regiments could have echoed the colonel of the 12th when he wrote: "My regiment suffered severely in this attack." He concluded that "it was impossible for us to hold the position we had gained any longer without being cut to pieces or compelled to surrender, the enemy having advantage of us in numbers and position." O'Neal used almost the same language (his "we had gained" being the royal or editorial "we" apparently because he had not participated in the advance); much of the body of O'Neal's report is paraphrased noticeably from Colonel Pickens's report for the 12th Alabama.[53]

O'Neal's premature start and the all-too-brief duration of his attack combined to leave a dreadful situation facing Iverson's brigade, just to O'Neal's right. With no support on the left, and with the vulnerable Federal flank opposite O'Neal out of danger, the four North Carolina regiments that made up Iverson's command needed judicious and competent leadership. Instead, they had Alfred Iverson. The result was a disaster so awful that one survivor wrote feelingly: "Deep and long must the desolate homes and orphan children of North Carolina rue the rashness of that hour."[54]

Alfred Iverson, Jr., was thirty-four years old at Gettysburg. He had served as a lieutenant during the Mexican War while still in his teens, under a commission probably secured by the political influence of his father, a newly seated United States congressman. In 1855 the younger Iverson received a commission in the regular army directly from civilian life (by now his father was a United States senator, seated the same day as the son's commissioning date). In 1861, Alfred Iverson participated in raising the 20th North Carolina Infantry and became its first colonel.

The North Carolina regiment apparently never enjoyed the empathy with its first commander that developed under like circumstances in so many other units. The officers of the 20th spent the entire winter before Gettysburg at loggerheads with Iverson, who had recently been promoted to command the brigade. The field officers of Iverson's old regiment did not like him, and he reciprocated the feeling. A captain in the 20th wrote in January, "Genl Iverson now and all ways did hate Major [Nelson] Slough." When the brigadier sought to import a friend from outside the regiment to take the colonelcy that he himself had vacated, twenty-six officers of the 20th signed a protest to Confederate Adjutant and Inspector General Samuel Cooper. Iverson refused to forward the document. The rebellious officers sent it on anyway, "over hiss head"; perhaps the "hiss" served as editorial comment, rather than just indicating an anomalous Carolinian spelling.

On December 27, 1862, Iverson sent an aide to the camp of his old regiment to arrest all twenty-six of its officers. One of them, Captain (later major and lieutenant colonel) John Stanley Brooks, wrote an outraged letter home insisting that resistance to Iverson was every reasonable man's duty and

Brigadier General Alfred Iverson, Jr.
(Miller's *Photographic History of the Civil War*)

asserting that he would oppose him again "with grate plea-
sure" if occasion offered. Brooks considered resigning, and perhaps others did as well. The arrested men retained a high-
powered bevy of counsel, including Colonel (later brigadier
general) Alfred Moore Scales and Colonel William P. Bynum,
who would become a member of the state supreme court.

Iverson failed in his attempt to import an outside favorite
to command the 20th, but he took revenge on his irreverent
subordinates by convening a "diabolical board" (Brooks's
phrase, from two separate letters) that rejected promotions of
all who had opposed him.[55] The suffering officers of the 20th
would find relief from Iverson when he was exiled from the
army, but first they faced their worst ordeal of the war at
Gettysburg, where their misgivings about their chief found
ample validation.

Rodes intended that Iverson should attack simultaneously
with O'Neal and along the same axis. Neither of those intentions bore fruit. Iverson later reported that when he received
his advance orders, he at once sent a staff officer to watch for
O'Neal's movement so as to conform to it. Almost immediately the aide returned with the startling word that O'Neal already was moving. The poor timing resulted in O'Neal's
repulse "just as we came up," according to one of the North
Carolinians. Division commander Rodes reported bluntly that
Iverson's heavy loss came because of his "left being thus exposed." Although Iverson's official declaration that the Alabamians had been "almost instantaneously driven back" was
an exaggeration, the brevity of O'Neal's ill-aimed effort did ensure a failure of collaboration. Even misdirected and understrength as it was, the Alabama brigade's attack would have
served to ease Iverson's plight had it been pressed with ordi-
nary tenacity.[56]

The four North Carolina regiments—5th, 20th, 23d, and
12th, from left to right—began their advance heading more
south than east. Nearly fifteen hundred officers and men
marched with the doomed brigade. Losses at Chancellorsville
had left some regiments short on officers. The 5th, for instance, had no field officers present and lost the captain

commanding and the other three captains on duty on July 1 to wounds. The major and lieutenant colonel of the 20th were hit "soon" after the advance began, each wounded in his left arm, leaving that hard-pressed regiment critically short of leadership.[57] (The scarcity of officers with Iverson and the frightful losses among those who were present show up in a historiographical fashion as clearly as on the battlefield: accounts of the regiment's actions by officers are uncommonly scarce.)

The most critical leadership shortfall in the Forney fields is chargeable to Alfred Iverson. A member of the 23d wrote pointedly: "But our brigade commander (Iverson) after ordering us forward, did not follow us in that advance, and our alignment soon became false. There seems to have been utter ignorance of the [enemy] force crouching behind the stone wall." A soldier of Ramseur's brigade, the division reserve, declared that Iverson "was drunk, I think, and a coward besides," and that the general "was off hiding somewhere." Lieutenant General Ewell's favorite staff officer (his stepson) wrote that he learned from Rodes, Daniel, and others of "the well-known cowardly behavior of Iverson."[58] For whatever reason, Iverson emulated O'Neal by remaining behind while his men attacked. He was not far enough to the rear to warrant the description "off hiding somewhere," though, because he soon found opportunity to embarrass himself by a humiliating misinterpretation of the behavior of his men as they closed with the enemy.

The field across which "unwarned, unled as a brigade, went forward Iverson's deserted band to its doom" was completely devoid of cover. Farmer Forney later described his crop on the field as "a luxuriant growth of Timothy." A member of the 97th New York who watched the approach of the unsuspecting North Carolinians wrote of a "crop of wheat" on an area that "was all open meadow in my front." The Carolinians aimed at the southeast corner of the field, where Federals were visible in the woods, unaware of the more potent enemy lurking closer to them, on their left front. The Northern brigades of Baxter and Paul in the Hook occupied a position that should have been very vulnerable to O'Neal; but to a force advancing as Iverson's was, Baxter and Paul held impregnable ground. A stone fence ran down the front about two-thirds of the distance from the Mummasburg Road to the woods. For part of the way, a wooden fence augmented the stones. The steep-edged ridge that made their right and rear so easily turned also made the front of the Federal regiments strong and secure. Between the rock fence and the steep ridge edge, the Federals found complete cover. "Not one of them was to be seen," a member of the 12th North Carolina recalled ruefully.⁵⁹

Iverson's men marched southeastward "as evenly as if on parade," one of them insisted. A Pennsylvanian waiting for orders to shoot at them agreed that "Iverson's men, with arms at a right shoulder, came on in splendid array, keeping step with an almost perfect line . . . as orderly as if on brigade drill, while behind the stone wall the Union soldiers, with rifles cocked and fingers on the triggers, waited and bided their time, feeling confident."⁶⁰ The men behind the stones had ample reason for confidence: the Carolinians were marching steadily, without skirmishers and without reconnaissance, into one of the most devastating deadfalls of the entire war.

The savage shock that awaited Iverson's men doubtless is beyond imagining for anyone who did not experience it. "When we were in point blank range," one of the victims later wrote, "the dense line of the enemy rose from its protected lair and poured into us a withering fire." At a range of little more than one hundred yards the Federals hurled "a sheet of fire and smoke . . . from the wall, flashing full in the faces of the Confederates, who at once halted, and, though their men were falling like leaves in a storm . . . attempted to make a stand and return the bitter fire." Situated as they were, the Carolinians could not stand for long. Most of them huddled under the fragile shelter of a shallow swale running irregularly through the field about eighty yards from the wall (a forward marker to the 88th Pennsylvania stands there today). They kept up what a Federal called "a rapid fusilade," but with scant success.⁶¹

The deadly effects of the initial surprise seemed to onlookers to be the worst part of the ordeal. One of Ramseur's men watching from back up the ridge wrote that when "Iverson's men charged . . . the Yankees raised up and fired and the death rate was terrible." Down near the wall, the initial horror soon developed into an even more gruesome scene as the helpless Confederates fell in long windrows. "I believe every man who stood up was either killed or wounded," an officer in the 20th North Carolina wrote. Not far to his right, an officer of the 23d saw so much carnage that he later insisted to a comrade "that it was the only battle—and he was in all in which the command was engaged from Williamsburg to Appomattox—where the blood ran like a branch. And that too, on the hot, parched ground."[62]

A Virginia artillerist who passed the Forney fields just a few hours later noticed with surprise and shock that the butchered Carolinians had fallen so thickly and quickly that they lay in perfect alignment. The gunner counted, within "a few feet . . . seventy-nine (79) North Carolinians laying dead in a straight line." The ghastly formation "was perfectly dressed. Three had fallen to the front, the rest had fallen backward; yet the feet of all these dead men were in a perfectly straight line." The "perfectly sickening and heart-rending" sight prompted the Virginian to exclaim: "Great God! When will this horrid war stop?"[63]

Alfred Iverson watched this bloody horror from some point well to the rear and understood it so imperfectly that he committed what Ewell in his official report called "the unfortunate mistake of . . . at this critical juncture . . . sending word to Major-General Rodes that one of his regiments had raised the white flag and gone over to the enemy." Iverson described the incident as resulting from seeing his men lying down in front of the Federal wall. In his official report the general backed away earnestly from his confused judgment of July 1, writing: "When I found afterward that 500 of my men were left lying dead and wounded on a line as straight as a dress parade, I exonerated, with one or two disgraceful exceptions, the survivors. . . . No greater gallantry and heroism has been displayed during this war."[64]

Absolution from their far-distant brigadier cannot have been of any current interest to the Carolinians bleeding in the swale, if in fact any of them ever considered Iverson in a position to pass judgment on anything they did. The historian of the 23d characterized their plight: "Unable to advance, unwilling to retreat, the brigade lay down in this hollow or depression in the field and fought as best it could." In the process, he noted, every one of the 23d's commissioned officers fell, with a single exception. So totally were the Confederates overwhelmed that they could put up little resistance when Federals swarmed out of the cover of their strong position and rushed through the swale gathering prisoners "with bayonets and clubbed muskets." As an enlisted man in the 23d put it, he and his comrades moved into battle "just in time for them to forge us in the rear of the line. We left the battle ground with only 60 men." Another member of the 23d explained the result in a letter home: "We fought like tigers and [made the] bravest stand I ever saw but the Yankees cross fired on us a good while and then . . . the Yankees ran up and captured very nearly all of them."[65]

Northerners firing their rifles down into the swale began shouting to one another about the need to charge out and gather in prisoners after Confederates began waving handkerchiefs tied to their guns as tokens of surrender. As the Federals scurried out to the swale and beyond, "several hundred of the rebs left their arms on the ground and rushed through our lines and they were directed to run out of range as quick as possible which they did without much urging." The momentum of their lunge into the swale carried some of the Federals on beyond into range of the Confederate brigades that soon would win the day on Oak Ridge. General Baxter—unlike Iverson and O'Neal, he was with his troops—shouted orders "to give them the cold steel," but a "scorching fire" quickly extinguished that notion.[66]

The only sizable piece of Iverson's brigade that escaped with any organizational integrity was the 12th North Carolina. Because the brigade line was angled away from the Federal position, the 12th on the far right suffered least from the deadfall and enjoyed the best opportunity to defend itself and to pull back from the trap. It suffered fewer than half as many casualties as any of the other three regiments. Captain Don P. Halsey of Iverson's staff—the same aide who had arrested twenty-six officers of the 20th North Carolina for his chief the preceding December—stood in for the absent brigade commander and rallied the 12th and other such fragments as he could find. When Confederate reinforcements under competent leaders appeared, as they did very promptly, Halsey seized a battle flag and led Iverson's pathetic remnant in the victorious pursuit that had seemed impossible when the brigade blundered into the swale. Ewell went so far as to declare that Captain Halsey had "assumed command" in place of Iverson.[67]

The soldiers of Iverson's brigade immediately heard and repeated the prevalent account that their general "not only remained in the rear but that a big chestnut log intervened between him and the battle and that more than once he reminded his staff that for more than one at the time to look over was an unnecessary exposure of person." The brigade's regimental officers shared the feelings of the men about Iverson. Colonel Daniel Harvey Christie of the 23d North Carolina, suffering from a mortal wound and accordingly immune to concerns about rank or discipline, "had the surviving handful of the 23d" brought to the front yard of the house where he lay. From the porch the dying colonel "with much feeling assured them that he might never live to again lead them [into] battle but he would see that 'The Imbecile Iverson never should.' "[68]

In the aftermath of Gettysburg, participants and commentators reached an easy consensus on Iverson's disaster: they blamed the general and exonerated the men, accepting Rodes's verdict that the soldiers "fought and died like heroes." A staff officer repeating what he had heard from Rodes and others wrote soon after the war with disgust that although Iverson "was relieved at once & sent back to await trial," he fell into the hands of politicians when "forwarded to Richmond, got off scot free & had a brigade of reserves given him in Georgia." Thomas F. Toon, a colonel of the 20th who won promotion to brigadier general late in the war, bitterly summarized Iverson's disaster at Gettysburg in a succinct phrase opening his sketch of the regiment: "initiated at Seven Pines, sacrificed at Gettysburg, surrendered at Appomattox."[69]

The historian of the 12th North Carolina recorded the sorrowful burial of the dead who strewed the swale in number far too large and an equally melancholy visit to the scene years after the war:

> In the lowest part of the depression, in the rear of the battleground of Iverson's Brigade, four shallow pits were dug by the prisoners, in which were buried the dead of that brigade. The surface of these pits is to be easily distinguished [to] this day [ca. 1900] from surrounding ground on account of the more luxuriant growth of the grass and crops over them. Mr. Forney, who owned the ground on which the battle was fought, and who still owns it, and the writer of this sketch, two years ago, with pointers in their hands, traced with ease and certainty the edges of these pits as they walked around them. Mr. Forney said that the place was then known, throughout the neighborhood, as the "Iverson Pits," and that for years after the battle there was a superstitious terror in regard to the field, and that it was with difficulty that laborers could be kept at work there on the approach of night on that account.[70]

Iverson's disaster ended Confederate fumbling on Oak Ridge. In quick aftermath, Junius Daniel and Dodson Ramseur skillfully led their North Carolina brigades to triumph on precisely the same ground. George Doles held onto his stanchion firmly and well until Jubal A. Early's division poured down on his left and sealed a Confederate victory that swept the fields west of Gettysburg with irresistible force.

The three Confederate brigades that had suffered so badly on July 1 faced continued buffeting from fate during the rest of the campaign. When O'Neal's 3d Alabama sought to accompany Ramseur, he responded, "Yes, N.C. will stay with you"; an Alabamian discouraged by recent events replied, "They haven't been a doing it." The 3d and Ramseur soon stood together in the triumphant moment near where Iverson and O'Neal had failed so signally. On July 2 the Alabama brigade moved into the confused fighting around Culp's Hill and played a secondary role that is apparently impossible to decipher in detail at this late date. Its difficult outing in Pennsylvania continued during the retreat from Gettysburg. In a frustrating anticlimax to the bitter main event, the brigade's quartermaster trains fell prey to Yankee cavalry at 2 A.M. on July 5. Among the losses was a money chest holding some $11,235 scheduled for paying the troops and feeding them.[71]

Joseph Davis's shattered brigade was included for some reason in the assault on Cemetery Ridge on July 3. Perhaps the arrival of the full-strength 11th Mississippi contributed to the decision to subject the brigade to further battering. Iverson's brigade was beyond further service. Rodes's division as a whole cut a surprisingly faint figure after leaving Oak Ridge. O'Neal's son and namesake, who served on Rodes's staff at Gettysburg (but doubtless felt his father's humiliation deeply), declared that the division "could easily have taken possession of the hill which afterward sent such havoc through our Army, but [was] prevented by our Division Commander." A field officer of the Alabama brigade commented pointedly about the poor coordination of Confederate efforts at Gettysburg. "From the first day reason seemed to have deserted our generals," he wrote. Each division general seemed bent on "acting on his own hook" and "without the smallest concert of action with the other Division Commanders." "So lamentably conspicuous was this want of concert," he insisted, "that the privates noticed it and when ordered to charge did so with misgivings as to the result."[72]

The affairs on Oak Ridge constituted a series of extraordinarily dark tactical failures in the midst of a Confederate strategic bonanza. They supplied renewed evidence of the military truth that leaders must lead, rather than rely on direction from ivory towers. The disasters also established some trends only clearly visible with hindsight: Ewell was not Stonewall Jackson in fact or even in simulacrum; the Robert Rodes of July 1863 was not the Robert Rodes of 1864; Iverson, O'Neal, and Davis were not competent and never would be. The aftermath of the disasters gave further evidence that Ramseur was as able as he had seemed to be and new evidence that Daniel brought solid competence to the army he had recently joined.

When he reflected on Gettysburg a few years later, R. E. Lee doubtless had July 1 clearly in mind when he commented on the absence—for very different reasons—of two crucial officers. "Stuart failed to give him information," Lee told a former staff officer, "and this deceived him into a general battle." And, Lee mused, he "often thinks that if Jackson had been there he would have succeeded."[73]

Appendix

Headquarters, *June* 22, 1863

Maj. Gen. J. E. B. STUART,

Commanding Cavalry:

GENERAL: I have just received your note of 7.45 this morning to General Longstreet. I judge the efforts of the enemy yesterday were to arrest our progress and ascertain our whereabouts. Perhaps he is satisfied. Do you know where he is and what he is doing? I fear he will steal a march on us, and get across the Potomac before we are aware. If you find that he is moving northward, and that two brigades can guard the Blue Ridge and take care of your rear, you can move with the other three into Maryland, and take position on General Ewell's right, place yourself in communication with him, guard his flank, keep him informed of the enemy's movements, and collect all the supplies you can for the use of the army. One column of General Ewell's army will probably move toward the Susquehanna by the Emmitsburg route; another by Chambersburg. Accounts from him last night state that there was no enemy west of Frederick. A cavalry force (about 100) guarded the Monocacy Bridge, which was barricaded. You will, of course, take charge of [A. G.] Jenkins' brigade, and give him necessary instructions. All supplies taken in Maryland must be by authorized staff officers for their respective departments—by no one else. They will be paid for, or receipts for the same given to the owners. I will send you a general order on this subject, which I wish you to see is strictly complied with.

I am, very respectfully, your obedient servant

R. E. LEE

General.

Headquarters,

Millwood, June 22, 1863—7 p.m.

Maj. Gen. J. E. B. STUART,

Commanding Cavalry:

GENERAL: General Lee has inclosed to me this letter to you,* to be forwarded to you, provided you can be spared from my front, and provided I think that you can move across the Potomac without disclosing our plans. He speaks of your leaving, via Hopewell Gap, and passing by the rear of the enemy. If you can get through by that route, I think that you will be less likely to indicate what our plans are than if you should cross by passing to our rear. I forward the letter of instructions with these suggestions.

Please advise me of the condition of affairs before you leave, and order General Hampton—whom I suppose you will leave here in command—to report to me at Millwood, either by letter or in person, as may be most agreeable to him.

Most respectfully,

JAMES LONGSTREET,

Lieutenant-General.

N. B.—I think that your passage of the Potomac by our rear at the present moment will, in a measure, disclose our plans. You had better not leave us, therefore, unless you can take the proposed route in rear of the enemy.

Headquarters Army of Northern Virginia,

June 23, 1863—5 p.m.

Maj. Gen. J. E. B. STUART,

Commanding Cavalry:

GENERAL: Your notes of 9 and 10.30 a.m. to-day have just been received. As regards the purchase of tobacco for your men, supposing that Confederate money will not be taken, I am willing for your commissaries or quartermasters to purchase this tobacco and let the men get it from them, but I can have nothing seized by the men.

If General Hooker's army remains inactive, you can leave two brigades to watch him, and withdraw with the three others, but should he not appear to be moving northward, I think you had better withdraw this side of the mountain to-morrow night, cross at Shepherdstown next day, and move over to Fredericktown.

---

*Of same date.

You will, however, be able to judge whether you can pass around their army without hinderance, doing them all the damage you can, and cross the river east of the mountains. In either case, after crossing the river, you must move on and feel the right of Ewell's troops, collecting information, provisions, &c.

Give instructions to the commander of the brigades left behind, to watch the flank and rear of the army, and (in the event of the enemy leaving their front) retire from the mountains west of the Shenandoah, leaving sufficient pickets to guard the passes, and bringing everything clean along the Valley, closing upon the rear of the army.

As regards the movements of the two brigades of the enemy moving toward Warrenton, the commander of the brigades to be left in the mountains must do what he can to counteract them, but I think the sooner you cross into Maryland, after to-morrow, the better.

The movements of Ewell's corps are as stated in my former letter. Hill's first division will reach the Potomac to-day, and Longstreet will follow to-morrow.

Be watchful and circumspect in all your movements.

I am, very respectfully and truly, yours,

R. E. LEE
General.

Notes

R. E. Lee and July 1 at Gettysburg

1. Douglas Southall Freeman, ed., *Lee's Dispatches: Unpublished Letters of General Robert E. Lee, C.S.A., to Jefferson Davis and the War Department of the Confederate States of America, 1862–1865* (1915; rev. ed., ed. Grady McWhiney, New York: G. P. Putnam's Sons, 1957), xxxvii.

2. Maj. Gen. Sir Frederick Maurice, ed., *An Aide-de-Camp of Lee, Being the Papers of Colonel Charles Marshall* (Boston: Little, Brown, 1927), 190. Although concerned with the overland campaign of 1864–65, Andrew A. Humphreys's discussion of the water route alternative illuminates the considerations affecting the choice of routes toward Richmond. See Humphreys, *The Virginia Campaign of '64 and '65: The Army of the Potomac and the Army of the James* (New York: Charles Scribner's Sons, 1883), 6–9.

3. Robert K. Krick, "Why Lee Went North," in Morningside Bookshop, *Catalogue Number Twenty-Four* (Dayton, Ohio, 1988), 10.

4. Edward Porter Alexander, *Fighting for the Confederacy: The Personal Recollections of General Edward Porter Alexander*, ed. Gary W. Gallagher (Chapel Hill: Univ. of North Carolina Press, 1989), 415.

5. U.S. War Department, *The War of the Rebellion: A Compilation of the Official Records of the Union and Confederate Armies*, 128 vols., (Washington, D.C.: GPO, 1880–1901), ser. I, vol. 27, pt. 3:932 (hereafter cited as *OR*; all references are to volumes in Series I); Clifford Dowdey and Louis H. Manarin, eds., *The Wartime Papers of R. E. Lee* (Boston: Little, Brown, 1961), 816.

6. *OR*, vol. 29, pt. 1:405; ibid., vol. 51, pt. 2:761; Dowdey and Manarin, eds., *Wartime Papers*, 675.

7. Dowdey and Manarin, eds., *Wartime Papers*, 388–89.

8. Ibid., 508.

9. Ibid., 843–44.

10. These data are taken from Thomas L. Livermore, *Numbers and Losses in the Civil War in America, 1861–65* (1901; reprint, Dayton, Ohio: Morningside House, 1986), 86, 88–89, 92, 98.

11. Krick, "Why Lee Went North," 11.

12. Richard E. Beringer, Herman Hattaway, Archer Jones, and William N. Still, Jr., *Why the South Lost the Civil War* (Athens, Ga.: Univ. of Georgia Press, 1986), 9, 16.

13. Lt. Col. George A. Bruce, "The Strategy of the Civil War," in *Papers of the Military Historical Society of Massachusetts*, 14 vols. and index (1895–1918; reprint, Wilmington, N.C.: Broadfoot Publishing Company, 1989–90), 13:469.

14. Maj. Gen. J. F. C. Fuller, *The Generalship of Ulysses S. Grant* (1929; reprint, Bloomington: Indiana Univ. Press, 1958), 365.

15. On the question of Northern morale in the early summer of 1864, see Lt. Col. Alfred H. Burne, *Lee, Grant and Sherman* (New York: Charles Scribner's Sons, 1939), 65, and William H. Swinton, *Campaigns of the Army of the Potomac: A Critical History of Operations in Virginia, Maryland and Pennsylvania, from the Commencement to the Close of the War, 1861–1865* (New York: Charles Scribner's Sons, 1882), 494–95. Swinton's perceptive study argued that after Cold Harbor the outlook in the North was so gloomy "that there was at this time great danger of a collapse of the war. The history of this conflict truthfully written will show this."

16. *OR*, vol. 27, pt. 2:308; Herman Hattaway and Archer Jones, *How the North Won: A Military History of the Civil War* (Urbana: Univ. of Illinois Press, 1983), 398.

17. Dowdey and Manarin, eds., *Wartime Papers*, 505; *OR*, vol. 27, pt. 2:305.

18. *OR*, vol. 27, pt. 3:868–69; ibid., vol. 40, pt. 2:703.

19. Maurice, ed., *Aide-de-Camp of Lee*, 73, 68.

20. Fuller, *Generalship of Grant*, 377.

21. *OR*, vol. 27, pt. 2:316; Maurice, ed., *Aide-de-Camp of Lee*, 217.

22. *OR*, vol. 27, pt. 2:313.

23. Ibid., 295–97.

24. Ibid., pt. 3:913, 931.

25. Edwin B. Coddington, *The Gettysburg Campaign: A Study in Command* (New York: Charles Scribner's Sons, 1968), 594–95.

26. *OR*, vol. 27, pt. 3:913. Lee's orders to Stuart and Longstreet's transmittal letter are reproduced in the Appendix.

27. *OR*, vol. 27, pt. 3:915.

28. It is apparent that the word "not" was unintended. Read literally, the orders of June 23 set forth different movements for Stuart depending on the same facts: "if General Hooker's army remains inactive" and "should he [Hooker] not appear to be moving northward." This almost certainly represented a careless ambiguity, but it seems not to have been a critical one. In both of the orders printed in the *Official Records*, Stuart was to feel Ewell's right and give him information. Virtually all writers have ignored this seemingly misplaced "not" in Lee's instructions to Stuart. An exception is Coddington, who in *The Gettysburg Campaign*, 108, overlooks the possibility of a simple error and speculates that perhaps Lee "considered it possible that Hooker would move southward to threaten Richmond, in which case Stuart's occupation of Frederick, a town equidistant from Baltimore and Washington, would be an effective deterrent."

29. *OR*, vol. 27, pt. 3:923.

30. Maurice, ed., *Aide-de-Camp of Lee*, 208 n.

31. *OR*, vol. 27, pt. 2:207-8; Kenneth P. Williams, *Lincoln Finds a General: A Military Study of the Civil War*, 5 vols. (New York: Macmillan, 1949-59), 2:666.

32. Coddington, *Gettysburg Campaign*, 207; Maurice, ed., *Aide-de-Camp of Lee*, 191.

33. *OR*, vol. 27, pt. 2:308.

34. Ibid., 307; 607; Coddington, *Gettysburg Campaign*, 264.

35. *OR*, vol. 27, pt. 2:444.

36. Coddington, *Gettysburg Campaign*, 280; Walter H. Taylor, *Four Years with General Lee* (1877; reprint, Bloomington: Indiana Univ. Press, 1962), 280; A. L. Long, *Memoirs of Robert E. Lee: His Military and Personal History* (New York: J. M. Stoddart, 1886), 275-76; *OR*, vol. 27, pt. 2:348-49.

37. Coddington, *Gettysburg Campaign*, 309.

38. Alexander, *Fighting for the Confederacy*, 233-34.

39. Ibid., 234; *OR*, vol. 27, pt. 2:317.

40. These postwar recollections by John B. Gordon, Henry Kyd Douglas, James Power Smith, Isaac R. Trimble, Jubal A. Early, Walter H. Taylor, and others are cited in Douglas Southall Freeman, *Lee's Lieutenants: A Study in Command*, 3 vols. (New York: Charles Scribner's Sons, 1942-44), 3:92-102.

41. *OR*, vol. 27, pt. 1:721, 277, 283, 704, 758-59, 777, 825; Harry W. Pfanz, *Gettysburg—The Second Day* (Chapel Hill: Univ. of North Carolina Press, 1987), 38-39.

42. *OR*, vol. 27, pt. 2:555, 445.

43. Ibid., 470, 607, 445.

44. Freeman, *Lee's Lieutenants*, 3:97-98.

45. *OR*, vol. 27, pt. 2:317-18.

46. Freeman, *Lee's Lieutenants*, 3:90-105.

Confederate Corps Leadership on the First Day at Gettysburg: A. P. Hill and Richard S. Ewell in a Difficult Debut

1. Much of the controversial writing about Gettysburg appeared in the pages of J. William Jones et al., eds., *Southern Historical Society Papers*, 52 vols. and 2-vol. index (1876-1959; reprint, Millwood, N.Y.: Kraus Reprint Company, 1977-80) (hereafter cited as *SHSP*); see especially vols. 4-6 for the opening arguments by Jubal A. Early, James Longstreet, and other principals in the debate. Important modern works include Thomas L. Connelly, *The Marble Man: Robert E. Lee and His Image in American Society* (New York: Knopf, 1977), especially chaps. 2 and 3; Connelly and Barbara Bellows, *God and General Longstreet: The Lost Cause and the Southern Mind* (Baton Rouge: Louisiana State Univ. Press, 1982), especially chap. 1; Glenn Tucker, *Lee and Longstreet at Gettysburg* (Indianapolis: Bobbs-Merrill, 1968), which devotes considerable attention to Richard S. Ewell; William Garrett Piston, *Lee's Tarnished Lieu-*

tenant: James Longstreet and His Place in Southern History (Athens, Ga.: Univ. of Georgia Press, 1987); and Gaines M. Foster, *Ghosts of the Confederacy: Defeat, the Lost Cause, and the Emergence of the New South* (New York: Oxford Univ. Press, 1987), especially chaps. 3–7.

2. On the reorganization of the army and the importance of Jackson's legacy, see Freeman, *Lee's Lieutenants*, 2:683–714.

3. Spencer Glasgow Welch, *A Confederate Surgeon's Letters to His Wife* (1911; reprint, Marietta, Ga.: Continental Book Company, 1954), 66–67 (the 10th Virginia was in George H. Steuart's brigade of Edward Johnson's division); Henry Heth, "Letter from Major-General Henry Heth, of A. P. Hill's Corps, A.N.V.," in *SHSP* 4:155.

4. Jedediah Hotchkiss, *Virginia*, vol. 4 of Clement A. Evans, ed., *Confederate Military History* (1899; reprint, Wilmington, N.C.: Broadfoot Publishing Company, 1987), 403; Edward Porter Alexander, *Military Memoirs of a Confederate: A Critical Narrative* (1907; reprint, Dayton, Ohio: Press of Morningside Bookshop, 1977), 381; John S. Mosby, *Stuart's Cavalry in the Gettysburg Campaign* (1908; reprint, Gaithersburg, Md.: Olde Soldier Books, 1987), 141, 155.

5. Jennings C. Wise, *The Long Arm of Lee; or, The History of the Artillery of the Army of Northern Virginia, With a Brief Account of the Confederate Bureau of Ordnance*, 2 vols. (1915; reprint, Richmond, Va.: Owens Publishing Company, 1988), 2:615; Warren W. Hassler, *Crisis at the Crossroads: The First Day at Gettysburg* (University, Ala.: Univ. of Alabama Press, 1970), 153; Coddington, *Gettysburg Campaign*, 273–74; Freeman, *Lee's Lieutenants*, 3:170–71.

6. William Starr Myers, ed., "The Civil War Diary of General Isaac Ridgeway Trimble," *Maryland Historical Magazine* 17 (March 1922):11 (Trimble's use of "Cemetery Hill" and "Culp's Hill," local place names that he almost certainly did not know at the time of the battle, suggests that he revised his diary after the fact); Isaac R. Trimble, "The Battle and Campaign of Gettysburg, from the Original MS. Furnished by Major Graham Daves of North Carolina," in *SHSP* 26:123–24. A more dramatic version of the meeting between Ewell and Trimble is in Randolph H. McKim, "The Gettysburg Campaign," in *SHSP* 40:273.

7. Glenn Tucker, *High Tide at Gettysburg: The Campaign in Pennsylvania* (Indianapolis: Bobbs-Merrill, 1958), 186 (quoting Stikeleather's letter, which was published in the *Raleigh* [N.C.] *Semi-Weekly Standard* on August 4, 1863); W. H. Swallow (a pseudonym), "The First Day at Gettysburg," *Southern Bivouac*, N.S., 1 (December 1885):441–42.

8. Henry Kyd Douglas, *I Rode with Stonewall, Being Chiefly the War Experiences of the Youngest Member of Jackson's Staff from the John Brown Raid to the Hanging of Mrs. Surratt* (Chapel Hill: Univ. of North Carolina Press, 1940), 247; John B. Gordon, *Reminiscences of the Civil War* (New York: Charles Scribner's Sons, 1903), 154–55.

9. Transcript of conversation between R. E. Lee and William Allan, April 15, 1868, pp. 13–14, and February 19, 1870, p. 21, William Allan Papers, Southern Historical Collection, Wilson Library, University of North Carolina, Chapel

Hill, North Carolina (repository hereafter cited as SHC). An editorial note preceding the text of the transcripts states that the "conversations were held in General Lee's office, usually in the morning, and Colonel Allan made his memoranda the same day."

10. Robert E. Lee, Jr., *Recollections and Letters of General Robert E. Lee* (1904; reprint, Wilmington, N.C.: Broadfoot Publishing Company, 1988), 415–16. These quotations are as remembered by Cassius Lee's son Cazenove Lee, who passed them along to Robert E. Lee, Jr.

11. Freeman, *Lee's Lieutenants*, 3:172–73; Clifford Dowdey, *Death of a Nation: The Story of Lee and His Men at Gettysburg* (New York: Knopf, 1958), 152–53; Hassler, *Crisis at the Crossroads*, 155; Coddington, *Gettysburg Campaign*, 320–21. For a treatment of Ewell on July 1 that generally accepts the traditional interpretation (and differs markedly from the present essay), see Gary W. Gallagher, "In the Shadow of Stonewall Jackson: Richard S. Ewell in the Gettysburg Campaign," *Virginia Country's Civil War* 5 (1986):54–59.

12. A glaring example of Gordon's confident dissembling may be found on page 160 of his *Reminiscences of the Civil War*, where he states that "impartial military critics, after thorough investigation, will consider . . . [it] as established . . . [that] General Lee distinctly ordered Longstreet to attack early the morning of the second day" at Gettysburg. By the time Gordon wrote this in the early twentieth century, a mass of evidence, much of it from the pens of Lee's own staff, left little doubt that Lee had given Longstreet no such order.

13. Jubal A. Early, *The Campaigns of Gen. Robert E. Lee: An Address by Lieut. General Jubal A. Early, Before Washington and Lee University, January 19th, 1872* (Baltimore: John Murphy, 1872), 45. For some of the richest collections of postwar testimony by Confederate participants, see Robert Underwood Johnson and Clarence Clough Buel, eds., *Battles and Leaders of the Civil War,* 4 vols. (New York: Century, 1887) (hereafter cited as *B&L*); *The Annals of the War Written by Leading Participants North and South, Originally Published in the Philadelphia Weekly Times* (Philadelphia: Times Publishing Company, 1879); and the periodicals *The Land We Love* (published 1866–69), *Our Living & Our Dead* (published 1874–76), *Southern Bivouac* (published 1882–85), and *Confederate Veteran* (published 1892–1932).

14. See "Letter from General Winfield Scott Hancock," in *SHSP* 5:168–72 (quotation on page 168). Among the many Confederates who quoted Hancock to prove that Ewell should have mounted assaults against Cemetery Hill were John B. Gordon, *Reminiscences of the Civil War,* 156, and Fitzhugh Lee, *General Lee* (New York: D. Appleton, 1894), 272–73. As careful a student as Coddington, *Gettysburg Campaign,* 318, 320–21, states that Hancock's letter indicated that to "achieve complete success after smashing the Union positions north and west of the town the Confederates would have had to continue their drive through the streets and up Cemetery Hill without a letup." Jackson might have accomplished this, observes Coddington, but Ewell could not.

15. Lee to Jefferson Davis, October 2, 1862, in *OR*, vol. 19, pt. 2:643; Lee to Davis, May 20, 1863, ibid., vol. 25, pt. 2:810–11.

16. Lee to A. P. Hill, June 5, 1863, ibid., vol. 27, pt. 3:859–60.

17. Ibid., vol. 27, pt. 2:307.

18. J. S. D. Cullen to James Longstreet, May 18, 1875, quoted in James Longstreet, *From Manassas to Appomattox: Memoirs of the Civil War in America* (Philadelphia: J. B. Lippincott, 1896), 383; *OR*, vol. 27, pt. 3:943–44 (letter from Lee to Ewell dated June 28 should be dated June 29; see Coddington, *Gettysburg Campaign*, p. 189).

19. *OR*, vol. 27, pt. 2:607, 637; Henry Heth, "Letter from Major-General Henry Heth, of A. P. Hill's Corps, A.N.V.," in *SHSP* 4:157.

20. Louis G. Young, "Pettigrew's Brigade at Gettysburg, 1–3 July, 1863," in Walter Clark, ed., *Histories of the Several Regiments and Battalions from North Carolina in the Great War, 1861–'65*, 5 vols. (1901; reprint, Wendell, N.C.: Avera Press for Broadfoot's Bookmark, 1982), 5:116–17 (cited hereafter as *N.C. Regiments*); Heth, "Letter from Major-General Heth," 157; *OR*, vol. 27, pt. 2:607. A somewhat different version of the episode involving Hill, Heth, and Pettigrew appears in Henry Heth, *The Memoirs of Henry Heth*, ed. James L. Morrison (Westport, Conn.: Greenwood Press, 1974), 173. The memoirs were written in 1897, some twenty years after the letter published in *SHSP*.

21. Walter Kempster, "The Cavalry at Gettysburg," in Ken Bandy and Florence Freeland, comps., *The Gettysburg Papers*, 2 vols. (Dayton, Ohio: Press of Morningside Bookshop, 1978), 1:402; *OR*, vol. 27, pt. 2:607. In his paper, originally presented in 1913, Kempster quoted a postwar conversation between himself and Heth.

22. Lieutenant Colonel Arthur James Lyon Fremantle, an English officer accompanying Longstreet at Gettysburg, recorded his impressions of Hill about 4:30 that afternoon: "General Hill now came up and told me he had been very unwell all day, and in fact he looks very delicate" (Fremantle, *Three Months in the Southern States: April–June, 1863* [1863; reprint, Lincoln: Univ. of Nebraska Press, 1991], 254). Both of Hill's biographers make the excellent point that Hill would have accompanied Heth's advance on July 1 if he thought there was any chance of a major engagement. See William Woods Hassler, *A. P. Hill: Lee's Forgotten General* (Richmond: Garrett and Massie, 1962), 158–59; James I. Robertson, Jr., *General A. P. Hill: The Story of a Confederate Warrior* (New York: Random House, 1987), 215.

23. *OR*, vol. 27, pt. 2:607, 637; Taylor, *Four Years with Lee*, 92–93. Lee had told Ewell on the morning of July 1 that "he did not want a general engagement brought on till the rest of the army came up" (*OR*, vol. 27, pt. 2:444.) He likely communicated the same sentiment to Hill.

24. Taylor, *Four Years with Lee*, 93; Heth, *Memoirs*, 175; *OR*, vol. 27, pt. 2:348.

25. Taylor, *Four Years with Lee*, p. 93. Heth went to Lee rather than Hill for permission to continue the assaults when Robert Rodes's division of Ewell's corps appeared on the Federal right (Heth *Memoirs*, 175). Coddington discusses Heth's failure to go through channels (i.e., through Hill) in *Gettysburg Campaign*, 309. Hill's uncertain health and Heth's friendship with Lee might help

to explain the divisional commander's actions. Robertson, *General A. P. Hill*, 215, argues that Hill should not be held responsible for initiating the action between Heth and Buford, but he "did become culpable once Heth became locked in combat."

26. *OR*, vol. 27, pt. 2:317–18.

27. Fremantle, *Three Months*, 254; *OR*, vol. 27, pt. 2:607.

28. Welch, *Surgeon's Letters*, 66; Perrin's letter is reproduced in Milledge L. Bonham, Jr., ed., "A Little More Light on Gettysburg," *Mississippi Valley Historical Review* 24 (March 1938):523; Young, "Pettigrew's Brigade at Gettysburg," 121.

29. William Woods Hassler, "A. P. Hill at Gettysburg: How Did He Measure Up as Stonewall Jackson's Successor?", *Virginia Country's Civil War* 5 (1986):51.

30. For rumors about Jackson's deathbed preference for Ewell, see Douglas Southall Freeman, *R. E. Lee: A Biography*, 4 vols. (New York: Charles Scribner's Sons, 1934–36), 3:8; Freeman, *Lee's Lieutenants*, 2:690; William Dorsey Pender, *The General to His Lady: The Civil War Letters of William Dorsey Pender to Fanny Pender*, ed. William Woods Hassler (Chapel Hill: Univ. of North Carolina Press, 1965), 237.

31. *OR*, vol. 25, pt. 2:810; transcript of conversation between R. E. Lee and William Allan, March 3, 1868, p. 8, Allan Papers, SHC.

32. *OR*, vol. 27, pt. 2:443–44.

33. Ibid., 444–45, 468–69, 552–55. For examples of postwar claims that Ewell frittered away this crucial opportunity (all of which compare Ewell to Jackson in the most unfavorable terms), see Douglas, *I Rode with Stonewall*, 247; Gordon, *Reminiscences*, 154–56; and James Power Smith, "General Lee at Gettysburg. A Paper Read Before the Military Historical Society of Massachusetts, on the Fourth of April, 1905," in *SHSP* 33:143–44. Douglas and Smith had served on Jackson's staff.

34. George Campbell Brown Memoir, p. 57, Brown-Ewell Papers, Tennessee State Library and Archives, Nashville, Tennessee.

35. This and the two following paragraphs are based on ibid., 59–61.

36. *OR*, vol. 27, pt. 2:469–70. See also Early's account in Jubal A. Early, *Lieutenant General Jubal Anderson Early, C.S.A.: Autobiographical Sketch and Narrative of the War Between the States* (1912; reprint, Wilmington, N.C.: Broadfoot Publishing Company, 1989), 269–71, which conforms closely to his official report.

37. *OR*, vol. 27, pt. 2:555.

38. Ibid., 445; Jedediah Hotchkiss, *Make Me a Map of the Valley: The Civil War Journal of Stonewall Jackson's Topographer*, ed. Archie P. McDonald (Dallas: Southern Methodist Univ. Press, 1973), 157; John B. Gordon to "My own precious wife," July 7, 1863, Gordon Family Papers (MS 1637), University of Georgia Special Collections, Athens, Georgia.

39. Taylor, *Four Years with Lee*, 95–96.

From Chancellorsville to Cemetery Hill:
O. O. Howard and Eleventh Corps Leadership

1. John Tyler Butts, ed., *A Gallant Captain of the Civil War* (New York: F. Tennyson Neely, 1902), 67 (this is the memoir of Captain von Fritsch, a member of Colonel Leopold von Gilsa's staff); Louise W. Hitz, ed., *The Letters of Frederick C. Winkler, 1862–1865* (Madison, Wisc.: Privately printed, 1963), 51; Oliver Otis Howard, "Gen. O. O. Howard's Personal Reminiscences of the War of the Rebellion," *National Tribune*, June 12, 1884.

2. The best recent examination of the Eleventh Corps on May 2 is Donald C. Pfanz, "Negligence on the Right: The Eleventh Corps at Chancellorsville," in *The Morningside Notes* (Dayton, Ohio: Morningside Bookshop, 1984), 1–8.

3. Coddington, *Gettysburg Campaign*, 306; James S. Pula, *For Liberty and Justice: The Life and Times of Wladimir Krzyzanowski* (Chicago: Polish American Congress Charitable Foundation, 1978), 92; Alanson H. Nelson, *The Battles of Chancellorsville and Gettysburg* (Minneapolis: Privately printed by the author, 1899), 78.

4. Charles W. McKay, "Bushbeck's Brigade," *National Tribune*, October 8, 1908. The Twelfth Corps, part of which also was identified with Pope's army, suffered some of the same ostracism.

5. Carl Schurz, *The Autobiography of Carl Schurz*, abridged in one volume by Wayne Andrews (New York: Charles Scribner's Sons, 1961), 247–48.

6. Quoted in Alfred C. Raphelson, "Alexander Schimmelfennig: A German-American Campaigner in the Civil War," *Pennsylvania Magazine of History and Biography* 87 (April 1963):172.

7. *The Battle of Chancellorsville and the Eleventh Army Corps*, unattributed pamphlet (New York: G. B. Teubner, 1863), 43.

8. Schurz, *Autobiography*, 249–51.

9. Ibid., 252–54; Hitz, ed., *Winkler Letters*, 52 (first quotation); Pula, *For Liberty and Justice*, 73–74, 89 (second quotation).

10. Frank J. Welcher, *The Union Army, 1861–1865: Organization and Operations, The Eastern Theater* (Bloomington: Indiana Univ. Press, 1989), 459. The officers were Schurz and Adolph von Steinwehr.

11. Pula, *For Liberty and Justice*, 74; John A. Carpenter, *With Sword and Olive Branch: Oliver Otis Howard* (Pittsburgh: Univ. of Pittsburgh Press, 1964), 50.

12. Oliver O. Howard, "After the Battle," *National Tribune*, December 31, 1885; Carl Schurz, "The Battle of Gettysburg," *McClure's Magazine* 29 (July 1907):273; Charles W. Howard, "The First Day at Gettysburg," in Military Order of the Loyal Legion of the United States (hereafter cited as MOLLUS), Illinois Commandery, *Papers* 4 (Chicago: Cozzens & Beaton, 1907), 256.

13. William Simmers, *The Volunteers Manual* (Easton, Pa.: D. H. Neiman, 1863), 26–27 (first quotation); Francis C. Barlow to his mother and brothers, May 8, 1863, typescript in the collections of Gettysburg National Military Park (hereafter cited as GNMP) (second quotation).

14. Schurz, *Autobiography*, 259; Butts, ed., *Gallant Captain*, 74. Simmers, *Volunteers Manual*, 28, offers a different explanation for von Gilsa's arrest: at Middletown, Barlow "was frantic because our worthy brigade commander had dared to await orders from Major-General Howard (by whose order he had been detached), before acting on his [Barlow's] order to rejoin the division."

15. Stewart Sifakis, *Who Was Who in the Civil War* (New York: Facts on File, 1988), 421. Two good sources on Ames are Blanche Butler Ames, comp., *Chronicles from the Nineteenth Century* (Clinton, Mass.: Privately printed, 1957), and Blanche Ames, *Adelbert Ames, 1835–1933: General, Senator, Governor* (New York: Argosy-Antiquarian, 1964).

16. Sifakis, *Who Was Who*, 678–79; Ezra J. Warner, *Generals in Blue: Lives of the Union Commanders* (Baton Rouge: Louisiana State Univ. Press, 1964), 530–31; Adolphus F. Vogelbach, "Honor to Whom Honor Is Due," *National Tribune*, October 11, 1888; Adin B. Underwood, *The Three Years' Service of the Thirty-Third Mass. Infantry Regiment, 1862–1865* (Boston: A. Williams, 1881), 117.

17. Vogelbach, "Honor to Whom Honor Is Due"; Sifakis, *Who Was Who*, 146, 606; Pula, *For Liberty and Justice*, 73; Francis C. Barlow to his mother and brothers, May 8, 1863, GNMP.

18. Schurz, *Autobiography*, passim; Sifakis, *Who Was Who*, 574; Warner, *Generals in Blue*, 426–28.

19. Raphelson, "Alexander Schimmelfennig," provides the best biographical treatment of its subject. See also Butts, ed., *Gallant Captain*, 70, and Pula, *For Liberty and Justice*, 58–59.

20. Pula's *For Liberty and Justice* is a full-length biography of Krzyzanowski. See page 59 for a discussion of Krzyzanowski's style of command.

21. Coddington, *Gettysburg Campaign*, 306.

22. Simmers, *Volunteers Manual*, 26. Although the evidence is often contradictory, many writers believe that morale in the Eleventh Corps improved rapidly after Chancellorsville. See, for example, Theodore A. Dodge, *The Campaign of Chancellorsville* (Boston: James R. Osgood, 1881), 104; Owen Rice, *Afield with the Eleventh Army Corps at Chancellorsville* (Cincinnati: H. C. Sherrick, 1885), 38; and Edwin B. Coddington, "The Role of the 153rd Pennsylvania Volunteer Infantry in the Civil War," copy of article from unidentified journal in Vertical File, GNMP.

23. Schurz, "Battle of Gettysburg," 272.

24. Pula, *For Liberty and Justice*, 91; Butts, ed., *Gallant Captain*, 71 (quotation).

25. Howard, "Gen. O. O. Howard's Personal Reminiscences," *National Tribune*, June 26 (quotation), July 3, 1884.

26. Albert Wallber, "From Gettsburg to Libby Prison," in MOLLUS, Wisconsin Commandery, *Papers* 4 (Milwaukee: Burdick & Allen, 1914), 191; Simmers, *Volunteers Manual*, 27; Andrew J. Boies, *Record of the Thirty-Third Massachusetts Volunteer Infantry* (Fitchburg, Mass.: Sentinel Printing Company, 1880), 31.

27. Carpenter, *Sword and Olive Branch*, 50; O. O. Howard, "Campaign and Battle of Gettysburg," *Atlantic Monthly Magazine* 38 (July 1876):51; Schurz, *Autobiography*, 255; Alfred E. Lee, "Reminiscences of the Gettysburg Battle," *Lippincott's Magazine*, N.S., 6 (July 1883):54.

28. Boies, *Thirty-Third Massachusetts*, 32; Edward S. Salomon, *Gettysburg* (San Francisco: Shannon-Conmy Printing Company, 1913), 5.

29. Howard, "Campaign and Battle of Gettysburg," 52; Pula, *For Liberty and Justice*, 93; Oliver Otis Howard, *The Autobiography of Oliver Otis Howard*, 2 vols. (New York: Baker and Taylor, 1908), 1:402; Schurz, "Battle of Gettysburg," 272.

30. *OR*, vol. 27, pt. 3:414–15; ibid., pt. 1:733, 739.

31. Charles Howard, "First Day at Gettysburg," 239; *OR*, vol. 27, pt. 1:701; Howard, "Gen. O. O. Howard's Personal Reminiscences," *National Tribune*, November 27, 1884; Howard, *Autobiography*, 1:402–3; O. O. Howard to Jacobs, July 23, 1864, photocopy in the collections of GNMP.

32. Howard, "Campaign and Battle of Gettysburg," 52.

33. Warren W. Hassler, "The First Day's Battle at Gettysburg," *Civil War History* 6 (September 1960):263; Howard, *Autobiography*, 1:408–9; Howard, "Campaign and Battle of Gettysburg," 53; *OR*, vol. 27, pt. 1:701; Hassler, *Crisis at the Crossroads*, 30; Marshall D. Krolick, "The Union Command: Decisions That Shaped a Battle," *Blue and Gray Magazine* 5 (November 1987):15.

34. Mark H. Dunkelman and Michael J. Winey, *The Hardtack Regiment: An Illustrated History of the 154th Regiment, New York State Infantry Volunteers* (Rutherford, N.J.: Fairleigh Dickinson Univ. Press, 1981), 71; Howard, "Gen. O. O. Howard's Personal Reminiscences," *National Tribune*, November 27, 1884; Howard *Autobiography*, 1:408–9; Alfred E. Lee, "The Eleventh Corps: The Disadvantages Under Which It Fought at Gettysburg," *Philadelphia Weekly Press*, January 26, 1887; Coddington, *Gettysburg Campaign*, 280.

35. Howard, *Autobiography*, 1:409; Charles Howard, "First Day at Gettysburg," 239–40. Coddington, *Gettysburg Campaign*, 268–69, affirms that Major William Riddle of Reynolds's staff first contacted Howard.

36. *OR*, vol. 27, pt. 1:701; Howard, *Autobiography*, 1:409; Howard, "Campaign and Battle of Gettysburg," 53; Howard, "Gen. O. O. Howard's Personal Reminiscences," *National Tribune*, November 27, 1884.

37. Howard, "Campaign and Battle of Gettysburg," 53; Howard, *Autobiography*, 1:409; *OR*, vol. 27, pt. 1:701.

38. Howard, *Autobiography*, 1:409–10; Howard, "Campaign and Battle of Gettysburg," 53.

39. See Coddington, *Gettysburg Campaign*, 702–3 n. 90, for a discussion of Howard's claim that he rather than Reynolds selected Cemetery Hill. J. Max Mueller, a member of von Steinwehr's staff, accorded the honor to his chief in "Hancock at Gettysburg: The Claim That He Selected the Battle-ground Disputed by a Staff Officer," *New York Times*, October 16, 1880.

40. Howard, "Gen. O. O. Howard's Personal Reminiscences," *National Tribune*, November 27, 1884; Howard, *Autobiography*, 1:411. See also *Army and*

Navy Journal, April 16, 1864, for a positive statement supporting Howard's selection of the positon. Identified only as "A.S.," the author of this statement probably was von Steinwehr.

41. Edward C. Culp, *The 25th Ohio Vet. Vol. Infantry in the War for the Union* (Topeka, Kan.: George W. Crane, 1885), 77.

42. Howard, "Campaign and Battle of Gettysburg," 54; Howard, *Autobiography,* 1:412; *OR,* vol. 27, pt. 1:701–2; Howard, untitled typescript of article from unidentified journal, p. 29, in the collections of GNMP (cited hereafter as Howard, "Untitled Typescript"). Charles Howard, "First Day at Gettysburg," 244, remembered Skelly's given name as William.

43. Howard, "Untitled Typescript," 30–31; Howard, *Autobiography,* 1:413; and Charles Howard, "First Day at Gettysburg," 244, all identify the messenger as Hall. In his report in *OR,* vol. 27, pt. 1:702, Howard mentions Riddle by name, while in "Campaign and Battle of Gettysburg," 54, he calls the officer "Biddle."

44. Hassler, *Crisis at the Crossroads,* 65.

45. *OR,* vol. 27, pt. 1:742; Pula, *For Liberty and Justice,* 95–96; Wallber, "From Gettysburg to Libby Prison," 191–92.

46. *OR,* vol. 27, pt. 1:727; Schurz, *Autobiography,* 256–57; James Beale, *The Statements of Time on July 1 at Gettysburg, Pa. 1863* (Philadelphia: James Beale Printer, 1897), 25–26.

47. D. Scott Hartwig, "The 11th Army Corps on July 1, 1863—'The Unlucky 11th.'" *Gettysburg Magazine* 2 (January 1990):35. Hartwig's work is by far the best tactical study of the Eleventh Corps on July 1.

48. Hartwig, "11th Corps on July 1," 33, 35. Other estimates vary: *OR,* vol. 27, pt. 1:151, counts 9,893 officers and men equipped and present for duty on June 30; Hassler, *Crisis at the Crossroads,* 64, puts Howard's strength at 9,500; John W. Busey and David G. Martin, *Regimental Strengths at Gettysburg* (Hightstown, N.J.: Longstreet House, 1982), 78, offers the figure of 8,477 Eleventh Corps Infantry engaged at Gettysburg.

49. The artillery of the Eleventh Corps was organized as follows: Battery G, Fourth U.S. Artillery, Lieutenant Bayard Wilkeson, six light 12-pounders; Battery I, First Ohio Artillery, Captain Hubert Dilger, four light 12-pounders; Battery K, First Ohio Artillery, Captain Lewis Heckman, four light 12-pounders; Battery I, First New York Artillery, Captain Michael Wiedrich, six 3-inch rifles; Thirteenth New York Independent Battery, Lieutenant William Wheeler, four 3-inch rifles (*OR,* vol. 27, pt. 1:747).

50. Howard, "Campaign and Battle of Gettysburg," 54; *OR,* vol. 27, pt. 3:702 (quotation). In *OR,* vol. 27, pt. 1:727, and "The Battle of Gettysburg," 274, Schurz credits First Corps divisional commander James Wadsworth rather than Doubleday with dispatching the information about a Confederate threat west of Gettysburg.

51. Charles Howard, "First Day at Gettysburg," 248; *OR,* vol. 27, pt. 1:702. In his *Autobiography,* 1:416, Howard credited his brother with bringing news of Southern forces forming to the north.

52. *OR*, vol. 27, pt. 1:702; Hassler, "First Day's Battle at Gettysburg," 269–70; Coddington, *Gettysburg Campaign*, 282.

53. Joseph A. Gaston, "The Gettysburg Campaign, to include the Fighting on the First Day, July 1, 1863," umpublished paper (prepared at the Army War College, 1911–12), 72, U.S. Army Military History Institute, Carlisle Barracks, Pennsylvania (first quotation); Coddington, *Gettysburg Campaign*, 301 (second quotation); Louis Fischer, "At Gettysburg. First Day's Work of the Eleventh Corps, July 1, 1863." *National Tribune*, December 12, 1889.

54. Howard, "Untitled Typescript," 33.

55. Coddington, *Gettysburg Campaign*, 301–2.

56. Howard, "Campaign and Battle of Gettysburg," 55; Chapman Biddle, *The First Day of the Battle of Gettysburg: An Address Before the Historical Society of Pennsylvania, March 8, 1880* (Philadelphia: J. B. Lippincott, 1880), 39. In his *Autobiography*, 1:414, Howard states that he rode with Barlow "through the city, and out to what is now Barlow Hill"; however, no other source supports this claim. See Hartwig, "11th Corps on July 1," 39, for a discussion of how far Howard advanced.

57. Sidney G. Cooke, "The First Day at Gettysburg," in MOLLUS, Kansas Commandery, *War Talks in Kansas* (Kansas City, Mo.: F. Hudson, 1906), 282. Cooke served in the 147th New York Infantry.

58. Hassler, *Crisis at the Crossroads*, 68; Raphelson, "Alexander Schimmelfennig," 174; *OR*, 27, pt. 1:728.

59. *OR*, vol. 27, pt. 1:721; Hassler, *Crisis at the Crossroads*, 69.

60. Howard, "Campaign and Battle of Gettysburg," 56; Howard, *Autobiography*, 1:414; Coddington, *Gettysburg Campaign*, 282; Krolick, "Union Command," 17; *OR*, vol. 27, pt. 7:702–3; Hassler, *Crisis at the Crossroads*, 111.

61. *OR*, vol. 27, pt. 1:728; Schurz, "Battle of Gettysburg," 276 (quotation).

62. Hartwig disagrees in "11th Corps on July 1," 49, concluding that "there is not sufficient evidence to form a reasonable opinion." But see ibid., 43, which seems to ascribe the decision to Barlow after all.

63. Howard, *Autobiography*, 1:416.

64. Schurz, "Battle of Gettysburg," 276; Schurz, *Autobiography*, 259; *OR*, vol. 27, pt. 1:728; Francis C. Barlow to his mother, July 7, 1863, copy in the collections of GNMP; Butts, ed., *Gallant Captain*, 75; Edward C. Culp, "Gettysburg: Reminiscences of the Great Fight by a Participant," *National Tribune*, March 19, 1885.

65. Hartwig, "11th Corps on July 1," 40; Coddington, *Gettysburg Campaign*, 291; Fred Tilberg to Warren Hassler, January 16, 1951, Vertical File, GNMP.

66. Raphelson, "Alexander Schimmelfennig," 174, advances this theory, which is persuasive but unprovable. In "11th Corps on July 1," 40, Hartwig speculates that Barlow's motives were purely defensive.

67. Henry J. Hunt, "The First Day at Gettysburg," in *B&L*, 3:281; Hassler, *Crisis at the Crossroads*, 70; Hassler, "First Day's Battle at Gettysburg," 270;

Schurz, "Battle of Gettysburg," 276; *OR*, vol. 27, pt. 1:728; Schurz, *Autobiography*, 259.

68. Hartwig, "11th Corps on July 1," 43; George Campbell Brown, "My Confederate Experiences," typescript in the collections of GNMP.

69. Hartwig, "11th Corps on July 1," 43–44; Hassler, *Crisis at the Crossroads*, 88; Krolick, "Union Command," 18; Coddington, *Gettysburg Campaign*, 291. Krolick and Coddington characterize the Confederate assault as a surprise.

70. C. D. Grace, "Rodes's Division at Gettysburg," *Confederate Veteran* 5 (December 1897):614–15.

71. Hartwig, "11th Corps on July 1," 44–47, provides a detailed account of this phase of the fighting. See also Hassler, *Crisis at the Crossroads*, 81; quotation from Francis C. Barlow to his mother, July 7, 1863, GNMP.

72. Hunt, "First Day at Gettysburg," 281; G. W. Nichols, *A Soldier's Story of His Regiment and Incidentally of the Lawton-Gordon-Evans Brigade, Army of Northern Virginia* (1898; reprint, Kennesaw, Ga.: Continental Book Company, 1961), 116; Hartwig, "11th Corps on July 1," 45.

73. Hartwig, "11th Corps on July 1," 45; Lee, "Reminiscences," 56 (quotation).

74. Hartwig, "11th Corps on July 1," 45, 47.

75. *OR*, vol. 27, pt. 1:925. Buford transmitted this information to Meade via Alfred Pleasonton, commander of the cavalry in the Army of the Potomac.

76. Howard, "Campaign and Battle of Gettysburg," 56–57; Charles Howard, "First Day at Gettysburg," 253–56. In *Gettysburg Campaign*, 311–13, Coddington discusses Slocum's lack of activity.

77. *OR*, vol. 27, pt. 1:703; Howard, "Campaign and Battle of Gettysburg," 57 (quotation).

78. Hartwig, "11th Corps on July 1," 47; *OR*, vol. 27, pt. 1:703; Howard, *Autobiography*, 1:417.

79. Hartwig, "11th Corps on July 1," 47–48; Daniel B. Allen to J. B. Bachelder, April 5, 1864, copy in the collections of GNMP. Allen commanded the 154th New York of Coster's brigade; the 73d Pennsylvania was detached at the depot. See also Mark H. Dunkelman, "Coster Avenue Mural, Gettysburg," 4, typescript in the collections of GNMP.

80. Schurz, *Autobiography*, 260; Hartwig, "11th Corps on July 1," 48; Dunkelman and Winey, *Hardtack Regiment*, 72–73; John F. Sullivan, letter to the *Ellicotville* (N.Y.) *Post*, September 5, 1888, copy in the collections of GNMP.

81. Dunkelman and Winey, *Hardtack Regiment*, 75; Hartwig, "11th Corps on July 1," 48.

82. Schurz, *Autobiography*, 260 (first quotation); Dunkelman and Winey, *Hardtack Regiment*, 75 (second quotation); Dunkelman, "Coster Avenue Mural," 6; Mark H. Dunkelman, "Address at the Dedication of the Coster Avenue Mural, July 1, 1988," copy of unpublished address in the collections of GNMP.

83. *OR*, vol. 27, pt. 1:729.

84. Howard, "Campaign and Battle of Gettysburg," 57; Howard, *Autobiography*, 1:417; Hassler, "First Day's Battle at Gettysburg," 271; Charles Howard, "First Day at Gettysburg," 257–58; Hassler, *Crisis at the Crossroads*, 123. As is typical concerning times of day on a battlefield, the sources disagree as to when the Union army began its wholesale withdrawal. For example, Hartwig, "11th Corps on July 1," 49, states that the Eleventh Corps retreated "through the streets of Gettysburg" no later than 3:45 P.M.

85. James Beale, "Gettysburg: A Review of the Battle," *National Tribune*, January 1, 1885. It is possible that Beale referred to Barlow's rather than Schimmelfennig's division.

86. William F. Fox, ed., *New York Monuments Commission for the Battlefields of Gettysburg and Chattanooga: Final Report on the Battlefield of Gettysburg*, 3 vols. (Albany, N.Y.: J. B. Lyon, 1900, 1902), 1:380.

87. See, for example, *OR*, vol. 27, pt. 2:317 (R. E. Lee's report), 607 (A. P. Hill's report).

88. Schurz, *Autobiography*, 261; Underwood, *Three Years' Service*, 118; Culp, "Gettysburg Reminiscences."

89. Pula, *For Liberty and Justice*, 105; Coddington, *Gettysburg Campaign*, 295–96; Hunt, "First Day at Gettysburg," 283; Howard, "Gen. O. O. Howard's Personal Reminiscences," *National Tribune*, November 27, 1884; Underwood, *Three Years' Service*, 119.

90. Carl Schurz, *The Reminiscences of Carl Schurz*, 3 vols. (New York: McClure, 1907–8), 3:35–37; Butts, ed., *Gallant Captain*, 78; "The General's Tour," *Blue and Gray Magazine* 5 (November 1987):53; Fox, *Final Report on Gettysburg*, 3:25, 43; Raphelson, "Alexander Schimmelfennig," 176.

91. Hartwig, "11th Corps on July 1," 49.

92. Howard, "Campaign and Battle of Gettysburg," 58; Krolick, "Union Command," 17–18; Coddington, *Gettysburg Campaign*, 303.

93. Schurz, *Autobiography*, 261; *OR*, vol. 27, pt. 1:704; Culp, "Reminiscences." Some accounts state that Howard did not achieve effective control of the situation on Cemetery Hill until 5:00 P.M.

94. Charles Howard, "First Day at Gettysburg," 264, 258–59; Coddington, *Gettysburg Campaign*, 296–97; Howard, "Campaign and Battle of Gettysburg," 58 (quotations); Pula, *For Liberty and Justice*, 105, 107.

95. Hassler, *Crisis at the Crossroads*, 134; Schurz, "Battle of Gettysburg," 277; Hunt, "First Day at Gettysburg," 283; Schurz, *Autobiography*, 263.

96. Schurz, *Autobiography*, 264.

97. Krolick, "Union Command," 11–12, 19; Coddington, *Gettysburg Campaign*, 284–85; Howard, "Campaign and Battle of Gettysburg," 58; Howard, "Gen. O. O. Howard's Personal Reminiscences," *National Tribune*, November 27, 1884; Schurz, *Autobiography*, 262.

98. Eminel P. Halstead, "The First Day of the Battle of Gettysburg," in MOLLUS, District of Columbia Commandery, *Papers* 1 (Washington, D.C.: 1887), 7–8.

99. Howard, "Campaign and Battle of Gettysburg," 58–59; Howard, *Autobiography*, 1:418; *OR*, vol. 27, pt. 1:704; Howard, "Gen. O. O. Howard's Personal Reminiscences," *National Tribune*, November 27, 1884.

100. David M. Jordan, *Winfield Scott Hancock: A Soldier's Life* (Bloomington: Indiana Univ. Press, 1988), 83.

101. Beale, "Gettysburg," severely questions Howard's veracity on this and other points.

102. Schurz, *Autobiography*, 262–63.

103. *OR*, vol. 27, pt. 1:696–97.

104. Charles Howard, "First Day at Gettysburg," 264. In *OR*, vol. 27, pt. 1:705, and his *Autobiography*, 1:423, O. O. Howard gives slightly different versions of this exchange; he includes Slocum and Sickles as part of the group in *Autobiography*.

105. Schurz, *Autobiography*, 266.

106. Determining precise casualties is virtually impossible. The Eleventh Corps reported 3,801 casualties at Gettysburg (*OR*, vol. 27, pt. 1:183); Hartwig estimates 2,850 lost on July 1, including 250 killed, 1,200 wounded, and 1,400 missing and captured ("11th Corps on July 1," 49); Hassler, who provides casualties by regiment, gives the figures as 1,768 killed and wounded and 1,427 missing or captured for a total of 3,195 (*Crisis at the Crossroads*, 147–48).

107. Pula, *For Liberty and Justice*, 107, 101; *OR*, vol. 27, pt. 2:492 (first quotation); A. R. Barlow, "A Defense of the Eleventh Corps," *National Tribune*, January 15, 1885 (second quotation).

108. Francis C. Barlow to Robert Treat Paine, August 12, 1863, Francis C. Barlow to his mother, July 7, 1863, typescripts in the collections of GNMP.

109. Coddington, *Gettysburg Campaign*, 305; Hartwig, "11th Corps on July 1," 49; Hassler, *Crisis at the Crossroads*, 147–49.

110. O. O. Howard to his wife, July 16, 1863, copy in the collections of GNMP; D. Henson, "Ohio Troops in the Eleventh Corps," *National Tribune*, March 13, 1890; Robert Underwood Johnson and Clarence Clough Buel, "Hancock and Howard in the First Day's Fight," *B&L*, 3:289.

111. Charles Howard, "First Day at Gettysburg," 262.

112. Krolick, "Union Command," 17–18, 20, is Howard's most recent and eloquent critic. See also Coddington, *Gettysburg Campaign*, 300.

113. For a more sympathetic treatment of Howard's generalship, see Hassler, *Crisis at the Crossroads*, 154.

114. Schurz, *Autobiography*, 265; Howard, "Campaign and Battle of Gettysburg," 59.

Three Confederate Disasters on Oak Ridge:
Failures of Brigade Leadership on the First Day at Gettysburg

Robert K. Krick enjoyed invaluable archival assistance from the splendid historian of Gettysburg National Military Park, Kathy Georg Harrison, in doing the research for his article. Harrison's files include the unpublished John B. Bachelder maps (ca. 1883), which provide wonderfully detailed approximations of positions and movements on the first day at Gettysburg.

1. Samuel Merrifield Bemiss to "My dear Children," April 10, 1863, in the Bemiss Family Papers, Virginia Historical Society, Richmond, Virginia (MSS 1B4255d23). Bemiss was tending Lee because Lafayette Guild, the army's chief surgeon, was himself sick. Apparently unaware of the need to await postwar deification of Lee in some mythological process, Bemiss enthused in unbridled fashion about the character of his patient and hoped his children would some-day "imitate his actions and arrive at his excellencies."

2. W. W. Blackford, *War Years with Jeb Stuart* (New York: Charles Scribner's Sons, 1945), 230; T. Michael Parrish, ed., *Reminiscences of the War in Virginia, by David French Boyd* (Austin, Tex.: Jenkins, 1989), 19–21.

3. Louis G. Young, "Gettysburg Address," in *Addresses Delivered before the Confederate Veterans' Association, of Savannah, Ga., 1898–1902* (Savannah: Savannah Morning News Print, 1902), 35–36.

4. Heth, *Memoirs*, xli.

5. *OR*, vol. 25, pt. 2:633, 644–45.

6. Freeman, *Lee's Lieutenants*, 2:507.

7. *Official Register of the Officers and Cadets of the U.S. Military Academy* (New York: W. L. Burroughs, 1847), 7–8, 21; and publications of identical title and imprint dating from 1844, 1845, and 1846.

8. Henry Heth, *A System of Target Practice for the Use of Troops When Armed with the Musket, Rifle-Musket, Rifle, or Carbine. . . . Published by Order of the War Department* (Philadelphia: Henry Carey Baird, 1858). The reprint (Washington, D.C.: GPO, 1862) is identical, excepting the deletion of Heth's name, and probably was printed from the same plates.

9. J. W. Benjamin, "Gray Forces Defeated in Battle of Lewisburg," *West Virginia History* 20 (October 1958):32; Rose W. Fry, *Recollections of the Rev. John McElhenney, D.D.* (Richmond: Whittet & Shepperson, 1893), 181.

10. John A. Fite, *Memoirs of Colonel John A. Fite . . . 1832–1925* (N.p., 1935), 95.

11. *OR*, vol. 27, pt. 2:637; W. H. Bird, *Stories of the Civil War* (Columbiana, Ala.: Advocate Print, n.d.), 7–8.

12. Compiled Service Record of Joseph R. Davis in M331, Roll 72, National Archives, Washington, D.C.; L. M. Blackford to "My Dear Mother," March 11, 1863, in Blackford Family Papers (MS 1912), SHC. For an amusing, if minor, example of avuncular intervention, see the excuse for tardiness supplied by President Davis on behalf of General Davis in George L. Christian, "General Lee's Headquarters Records and Papers—The Present Location of Some of These," in *SHSP* 44:232–33.

13. J. E. B. Stuart to G. W. Custis Lee, December 18, 1862, Stuart Papers, Perkins Library, Duke University, Durham, North Carolina.

14. Robert K. Krick, *Lee's Colonels: A Biographical Register of the Field Officers of the Army of Northern Virginia*, rev. ed. (Dayton, Ohio: Press of

Morningside Bookshop, 1984), 43–44, 47, 83, 117, 172, 232, 242, 302, 310; John M. Stone to Joseph R. Davis, undated typescript in John B. Bachelder Papers, in the collections of GNMP.

15. *OR*, vol. 25, pt. 2:648–49.

16. Draft map for 11 A.M., July 1, compiled by John B. Bachelder, ca. 1883, revising his earlier published versions, in the collections of GNMP.

17. Dunbar Rowland, *The Official and Statistical Register of the State of Mississippi* (Nashville: Press of the Brandon Printing Company, 1908), 433.

18. Manuscript Bachelder map and bound volume containing Cope survey notes, p. 18, both in the collections of GNMP; John M. Stone to Joseph R. Davis, undated typescript in Bachelder Papers, GNMP.

19. Charles M. Cooke, "Fifty-Fifth Regiment," in *N.C. Regiments*, 3:297; Samuel Hankins, *Simple Story of a Soldier* (Nashville: Confederate Veteran, 1912), 43; LeGrand J. Wilson, *The Confederate Soldier* (Memphis: Memphis State Univ. Press, 1973), 116–17; J. V. Pierce (147th New York Infantry) to J. B. Bachelder, November 1, 1882, Bachelder Papers, GNMP (hereafter cited as Pierce letter, GNMP).

20. Hankins, *Simple Story of a Soldier*, 44; Wilson, *Confederate Soldier*, 117; Cooke, "Fifty-Fifth Regiment," 297.

21. *Galveston Daily News*, June 21, 1896, p. 1 (this article by a veteran of the 55th plagiarizes the account in *N.C. Regiments* but adds a few interesting personal notes); Pender, *The General to His Lady*, 244; Cooke, "Fifty-Fifth Regiment," 279; manuscript Bachelder map and bound volume containing Cope survey notes, p. 18, GNMP.

22. *OR*, vol. 27, pt. 2:650; W. B. Murphy (Co. A, 2d Mississippi Infantry) to F. A. Dearborn, June 29, 1900, copy in the collections of GNMP (this vivid and important source hereafter cited as Murphy letter, GNMP).

23. *OR*, vol. 27, pt. 2:649; Murphy letter, GNMP; Pierce letter, GNMP.

24. *Galveston Daily News*, June 21, 1896, p. 1; John M. Stone to Joseph R. Davis, undated typescript in Bachelder Papers, GNMP; Pierce letter, GNMP.

25. Cooke, "Fifty-Fifth Regiment," 297; Murphy letter, GNMP; Cope survey notes, p. 18, GNMP.

26. *OR*, vol. 27, pt. 2:649; Cope survey notes, p. 18, GNMP; John M. Stone to Joseph R. Davis, undated typescript in Bachelder Papers, GNMP.

27. Accounts by John A. Kellogg, A.A.G. of Cutler's brigade, and Dawes himself, in Bachelder Papers, GNMP, agree on the matter of the corking detachment.

28. Wharton J. Green, *Recollections and Reflections* (Raleigh: Edwards and Broughton, 1906), 176.

29. *Publications of the Mississippi Historical Society* 9 (1906):27; Murphy letter, GNMP.

30. Cooke, "Fifty-Fifth Regiment," 298.

31. Murphy letter, GNMP; Hankins, *Simple Story of a Soldier*, 47. For a splendid account of Federal operations against Davis, see D. Scott Hartwig, "Guts and Good Leadership: The Action at the Railroad Cut, July 1, 1863," *Gettysburg: Historical Articles of Lasting Interest* 1 (July 1989):5–14.

32. Wilson, *Confederate Soldier*, 118; R. T. Bennett, "Fourteenth Regiment," in *N.C. Regiments*, 1:719; John R. King, *My Experiences in the Confederate Army* (Clarksburg, W.Va.: Stonewall Jackson Chapter, United Daughters of the Confederacy, 1917), 13.

33. *OR*, vol. 27, pt. 1:638.

34. Henry Kyd Douglas manuscript marginalia in his copy of G. F. R. Henderson, *Stonewall Jackson and the American Civil War*, 2 vols. (London: Longmans, Green, 1898), 1:576, original in the collections of Antietam National Battlefield, Sharpsburg, Maryland.

35. James Power Smith to "My dearest sister," January 21, 1863, in the collections of Fredericksburg and Spotsylvania National Military Park, Fredericksburg, Virginia; Francis Smith Robertson, "Reminiscences of the Years 1861–1865," *Historical Society of Washington County, Va., Bulletin*, ser. 2, no. 23 (1986):15; Thomas H. Carter to D. H. Hill, July 1, 1885, in the Lee Papers, Virginia Historical Society; B. T. Lacy recollections, file folder titled Jackson's Staff, Roll 39, Jedediah Hotchkiss Papers, Library of Congress.

36. *OR*, vol. 27, pt. 2:552, 596.

37. James M. Thompson, *Reminiscences of Autauga Rifles* (Autaugaville, Ala: Printed for the author, 1879), 7; *OR*, vol. 27, pt. 2:552.

38. *OR*, vol. 27, pt. 2:602. The timing here, as for all other events under discussion, is from Bachelder's manuscript maps, ca. 1883, revising his earlier and less detailed published maps, originals in the collections of GNMP. The 1:00 P.M. map shows the three brigades abreast on the nose of Oak Ridge just above Forney's house.

39. *OR*, vol. 27, pt. 2:602, 592, 601, 553; Robert E. Park, "War Diary of Capt. Robert Emory Park, Twelfth Alabama Regiment, January 28th, 1863–January 27th, 1864," in *SHSP* 26:12–13.

40. *OR*, vol. 27, pt. 2:552.

41. R. E. Rodes to A. P. Hill, May 13, 1863, in Edward A. O'Neal's Compiled Service Record, Microcopy M331, Roll 190, National Archives; R. E. Lee to Jefferson Davis, May 26, 1863, in Freeman, ed., *Lee's Dispatches*, 95.

42. Circular letter in Edward A. O'Neal's Compiled Service Record; R. E. Rodes to Maj. W. H. Taylor, August 1, 1863, in Cullen A. Battle's Compiled Service Record, Microcopy M331, Roll 18, National Archives.

43. Edward A. O'Neal's Compiled Service Record.

44. R. E. Lee to Jefferson Davis, April 6, 1864, Lee to Secretary of War James A. Seddon, June 11, 1864, in Freeman, ed., *Lee's Dispatches*, 146–47, 225–26. O'Neal's letter of May 29, 1864, in his Compiled Service Record proposed the financial need criterion.

45. *OR*, vol. 27, pt. 2:553, 595–96.

46. W. H. May, "Reminiscences of the War Between the States," 5, typescript at the Georgia Department of Archives and History, Atlanta; *OR*, vol. 27, pt. 2:595–600, 592.

47. *OR*, vol. 27, pt. 2:553–54.

48. Ibid., 553; C. C. Wehrum to John B. Bachelder, January 21, 1884, Bachelder Papers, GNMP.

49. John D. Vautier, "At Gettysburg," *Philadelphia Press*, November 10, 1886.

50. *OR*, vol. 27, pt. 2:553, 601; Park, "War Diary," 13; Krick, *Lee's Colonels*, 267.

51. *OR*, vol. 27, pt. 2:553.

52. Ibid., 596–97, 603.

53. Ibid., 601, 592–93.

54. V. E. Turner and H. C. Wall, "Twenty-Third Regiment," in *N.C. Regiments*, 2:235.

55. John Stanley Brooks Letters (M-3094), SHC. Brooks's letters covering the controversy with Iverson include January 4, 1863, to "Dear Brother"; January 14, 1863, to "Dear Parrents"; March 1, 1863, to "Dear Sister"; and March 8, 1863, to "Dear Parrents and Sister M."

56. *OR*, vol. 27, pt. 2:579, 554; Turner and Wall, "Twenty-Third Regiment," 235–36.

57. Walter A. Montgomery, "Twelfth Regiment," in *N.C. Regiments*, 1:636; James C. MacRae and C. M. Busbee, "Fifth Regiment," ibid., 287; Turner and Wall, "Twenty-Third Regiment," 235; John Stanley Brooks to "Dear father," July 12, 1863, in Brooks Letters, SHC.

58. Turner and Wall, "Twenty-Third Regiment," 235; J. D. Hufham, Jr. [pseudonym], "Gettysburg," *Wake Forest Student* 16 (1897):454; George Campbell Brown memoir, p. 53, Brown-Ewell Papers, Tennessee State Library and Archives.

59. Turner and Wall, "Twenty-Third Regiment," 235; Montgomery, "Twelfth Regiment," 634–35; Isaac Hall to J. B. Bachelder, August 15, 1884, Bachelder Papers, GNMP.

60. Turner and Wall, "Twenty-Third Regiment," 235; Vautier, "At Gettysburg."

61. Vautier, "At Gettysburg."

62. Samuel D. Marshbourn Reminiscences, North Carolina State Archives; Thomas F. Toon, "Twentieth Regiment," in *N.C. Regiments*, 1:119; Turner and Wall, "Twenty-Third Regiment," 238.

63. Henry Robinson Berkeley, *Four Years in the Confederate Artillery* (Chapel Hill: Univ. of North Carolina Press, 1961), 50.

64. *OR*, vol. 27, pt. 2:444, 579–80.

65. Turner and Wall, "Twenty-Third Regiment," 236–37; J. L. Wallace Reminiscences, North Carolina State Archives; Jonathan Fuller Coghill to "Dear Pappy, Ma, and Mit," July 17, 1863, from a copy in the possession of John R. Bass, Spring Hope, North Carolina. Coghill's letters dated July 9, July 31, and August 1 (copies of which are in the possession of Mr. Bass) also supply details about the July 1 disaster.

66. C. C. Wehrum to John B. Bachelder, January 21, 1884, Bachelder Papers, GNMP; Vautier, "At Gettysburg."

67. Montgomery, "Twelfth Regiment," 635; Don P. Halsey, Jr., *A Sketch of the Life of Capt. Don P. Halsey of the Confederate States Army* (Richmond: Wm. Ellis Jones, 1904), 10–12; *OR*, vol. 27, pt. 2:445, 451, 554.

68. Memoir of Colonel Charles Christopher Blacknall by his son, in the Oscar W. Blacknall Papers, North Carolina State Archives.

69. *OR*, vol. 27, pt. 2:554; George Campbell Brown Memoir, p. 53, Brown-Ewell Papers, Tennessee State Library and Archives; Toon, "Twentieth Regiment," 111.

70. Montgomery, "Twelfth Regiment," 636–37.

71. May, "Reminiscences"; Compiled Service Record of Major James C. Bryan, Microcopy M331, Roll 38, National Archives. Bryan's papers include extensive transcripts from a court of inquiry that supply interesting material on the retreat, notably times of entry into various villages and routes taken by the trains.

72. Diary of Edward A. O'Neal, Jr., in John Coffee and Family Papers, Library of Congress; L. Minor Blackford, *Mine Eyes Have Seen the Glory* (Cambridge, Mass.: Harvard Univ. Press, 1954), 217–19.

73. Transcript of Conversation between William Allan and R. E. Lee, February 19, 1870, p. 21, William Allan Papers, SHC.

Bibliographic Essay

Readers should consult the endnotes for information about sources pertinent to the essays, but a few general suggestions for exploring the first day at Gettysburg seem appropriate. The best guide to the overall literature is Richard A. Sauers, comp., *The Gettysburg Campaign, June 3–August 1, 1863: A Comprehensive, Selectively Annotated Bibliography* (Westport, Conn., 1982). An essential collection of documents may be found in U.S. War Department, *The War of the Rebellion: A Compilation of the Official Records of the Union and Confederate Armies* (127 vols., index, and atlas; Washington, D.C., 1880–1901). Series 1, volume 27, parts 1–3 of the *Official Records* (known popularly as the *OR*) consists of three thick books containing reports, orders, and correspondence relating to Gettysburg. Postwar Union accounts are gathered in Ken Bandy and Florence Freeland, comps., *The Gettysburg Papers* (2 vols., Dayton, Ohio, 1978). *Gettysburg: Historical Articles of Lasting Interest* (Dayton, Ohio, 1989–), a biannual journal devoted solely to scholarly articles on the campaign, underscores Gettysburg's singular position among American military events.

The only modern treatment of the first day's fighting is Warren W. Hassler, Jr.'s brief *Crisis at the Crossroads: The First Day at Gettysburg* (Montgomery, Ala., 1970). Broader studies with considerable detail on the opening day include Edwin B. Coddington's magisterial *The Gettysburg Campaign: A Study in Command* (New York, 1968), Glenn Tucker's colorfully written but unreliable *High Tide at Gettysburg: The Campaign in Pennsylvania* (Indianapolis, 1958), and Clifford Dowdey's frankly pro-Southern *Death of a Nation: The Story of Lee and His Men at Gettysburg* (New York, 1958). *Gettysburg: The Confederate High Tide* (Alexandria, Va., 1985), by Champ Clark and the Editors of Time-Life Books, is the best pictorial history, while William A. Frassanito's *Gettysburg: A Journey in Time* (New York, 1975) supplies a fascinating array of period and modern photographs that pinpoint specific sites on the battlefield. Also useful for visitors to the field is Jay Luvaas and Harold W. Nelson, eds., *The U.S. Army War College Guide to the Battle of Gettysburg* (Carlisle, Pa., 1986). A trio of studies that focus on the Union side of the fighting west of Gettysburg are Alan T. Nolan's classic *The Iron Brigade: A Military History* (New York, 1961), Lance J. Herdegen and William J. K. Beaudot's massively detailed *In the Bloody Railroad Cut at Gettysburg* (Dayton, Ohio, 1990), and James L. McLean, Jr.'s *Cutler's Brigade at Gettysburg* (Baltimore, 1987), which chronicles the experiences of the Federal infantry that first engaged Confederates north of the Chambersburg Pike. A pair of superb Northern personal accounts are Rufus Dawes, *Service with the Sixth Wisconsin Volunteers* (1890; reprint, Madison, Wisc., 1962) and Stephen Minot Weld, *War Diary and Letters of Stephen Minot Weld, 1861–1865* (1912; reprint, Boston, 1979). On the Confederate side, G. W. Nichols's *A Soldier's Story of His Regiment (61st Georgia), and Incidentally of the Lawton-Gordon-Evans Brigade, Army of Northern Virginia* (1898; reprint, Kennesaw, Ga., 1961) presents vivid detail on the Southern assault north of Gettysburg, and Walter Clark, ed., *Histories of the Several Regiments and Battalions from North Carolina in the Great War 1861–65* (5 vols., 1901; reprint, Wendell, N.C., 1982) offers testimony from soldiers and officers in several units from North Carolina.

Three Union commanders who figured prominently in the events of July 1 wrote substantial accounts. Abner Doubleday's *Chancellorsville and Gettysburg* (1882; reprint, Wilmington, N.C., 1989) betrays the bitterness of a man who believed his services went largely unappreciated, while both special pleading and essential information mark O. O. Howard's *Autobiography of Oliver Otis Howard* (2 vols., New York, 1907–8) and Carl Schurz's ponderous *Reminiscences of Carl Schurz* (3 vols., New York, 1907–8). Among books by Confederate generals, John B. Gordon's famous and highly quotable *Reminiscences of the Civil War* (New York, 1904) should be used with care because of its sometimes casual regard for the truth; in contrast, Jubal A. Early's *Lieutenant General Jubal Anderson Early, C.S.A.: Autobiographical Sketch and Narrative of the War Between the States* (1912; reprint, Wilmington, N.C., 1989) displays a moderate tenor at odds with Early's reputation as a fierce Southern partisan.

Four biographies and a quartet of multivolume narrative histories also merit attention. Douglas Southall Freeman's *R. E. Lee: A Biography* (4 vols., New York, 1934–35) places the Southern chief in a decidedly favorable light; James I. Robertson, Jr.'s *General A. P. Hill: The*

Story of a Southern Warrior (New York, 1987) does the same for the commander of the Confederate Third Corps; Percy G. Hamlin's *"Old Bald Head": General Richard S. Ewell, Portrait of a Soldier* (1940; reprint, Gaithersburg, Md., 1988) chronicles its subject in straightforward fashion; and Edward J. Nichols's *Toward Gettysburg: A Biography of General John F. Reynolds* (University Park, Pa., 1958) finds little to criticize in Reynolds's conduct. Of the multivolume treatments, Shelby Foote's *The Civil War: A Narrative* (3 vols., New York, 1958–74) combines a graceful style and deft biographical touch. The finest history of the Army of Northern Virginia remains Douglas Southall Freeman's memorably written but sometimes biased *Lee's Lieutenants: A Study in Command* (3 vols., New York, 1942–44). *Glory Road* (Garden City, N.Y., 1952), the third volume in Bruce Catton's "Army of the Potomac Trilogy," reveals its author at his superlative best in describing battles through the eyes of participants; more scholarly and analytical is Kenneth P. Williams, *Lincoln Finds a General* (5 vols., New York, 1949–59), the second volume of which deals with Gettysburg.

The footnotes in these works point the way to hundreds of other pertinent sources on the opening day at Gettysburg—enough to satisfy all but the most voracious students.

Index

Jackson, Thomas J. "Stonewall," 41,
57, 92–93, 114–15, 139; as commander, 47; compared with suc-
cessors, 31–32, 34–37, 40, 94, 138;
correspondence with Lee, 95–96;
death of, ix; and Douglas, 39; in
the Shenandoah Valley, 97; and
von Gilsa's brigade, 79
Jenkins, Albert G., 14, 20, 141
Johnson, Edward, 27–28, 47, 49, 51,
53, 55, 112
Jones, Archer, 8, 10
Jones, J. William, 30
Jones, William E., 14, 20

Krick, Robert K., 2, 7
Krzyzanowski, Wladimir, 64, 71,
78–80, 84, 86

Lane, James H., 47
Law, Evander M., 102
Lee, Alfred E., 67, 73
Lee, Cassius, 36
Lee, Fitzhugh, 14, 30, 40, 50
Lee, G. W. C., 101
Lee, Robert E., vii, 3, 34, 64, 66–67,
122; and casualties, 7–9, 11–12; as
commander, 93; communications
with, 42; decision to invade Pa., 1,
2, 4, 10–13, 29; disappointment
with subordinates, 36–37, 56, 123,
139; grand strategy, 4–12; health,
93–94; and Heth, 95; with Hill in
battle, 44–45, 50; and Howard,
91–92; and Lost Cause, 39; orders
by, 53–54; praised, 159; reorganization of army, 31; use of cavalry,
14, 16–20, 141–43, 145; in western Va., 97
Lee, W. H. F., 14
Leesburg, Va., 14, 66
Lewisburg, Va., 97
Lincoln, Abraham, vii, 63–64

Little Round Top, viii
Long, Armistead L., 23
Longstreet, James, 4–5, 14–16, 19,
21, 23, 31, 40–42, 56, 141–43; role
in Gettysburg defeat, viii, 30
"Lost Cause" tradition, viii, 25, 39

McClellan, George B., 7, 58
McKay, Charles W., 81
McLean, Nathaniel C., 61, 63
McLean farm, 126, 128
McPherson's woods, 76
Madrid, Spain, 63
Magruder, William T., 101
Maine units: 2d Battery (Hall's),
106–7; 20th Infantry, 63
Malvern Hill, Va., 5
Manassas, Va., 5, 7, 40, 47, 66,
92, 108
Marksmanship, 96–97
Marshall, Charles, 2, 11–13, 17,
20, 21
Marsh Run, 68
Maryland campaign, 5, 12
Mason-Dixon Line, 69
Massachusetts units: 12th Infantry,
83, 126; 33d Infantry, 66–67, 83
Maurice, Frederick, 17
Meade, George G., 24, 32, 42,
68–69, 72, 76, 80, 85–87, 91;
and Howard, 87; respected by
troops, 67
Mechanicsville, Va., 5, 41
Mexican War, 129
Meysenburg, T. A., 70
Middleburg, Pa., 42
Millwood, Pa., 42
Milroy, Robert H., 115
Mississippi units: 2d Infantry,
101–2, 104–6, 108–9, 111; 11th
Infantry, 101–2, 138; 42d Infantry,
101–2, 104–6, 108–9
Monocacy, Md., 141
Morgan, John T., 122

The First Day at Gettysburg was composed in 10/12 Trump Medieval on a Xyvision system with Linotron 202 output by BookMasters, Inc.; printed by sheet fed offset on 60-pound Glatfelter Natural Smooth acid-free stock, Smyth sewn and bound over .088″ binders boards in ICG Arrestox B cloth, wrapped in dustjackets printed in two colors on 80-pound enamel stock with film lamination, also adhesive bound with paper covers printed in two colors on 12-point coated-one-side stock with film lamination by Braun-Brumfield, Inc.; designed by Will Underwood; and published by The Kent State University Press, Kent, Ohio 44242.

Contributors

GARY W. GALLAGHER is Head of the Department of History at Pennsylvania State University. He has published widely on the Civil War, including two previous books of essays edited for Kent State University Press—*Antietam: Essays on the 1862 Maryland Campaign* and *Struggle for the Shenandoah: Essays on the 1864 Valley Campaign.*

A. WILSON GREENE holds degrees in American History from Florida State University and Louisiana State University. Executive Director of the Association for the Preservation of Civil War Sites, he is the author of articles on various aspects of the Civil War as well as *J. Horace Lacy: The Most Dangerous Rebel of the County* and *"Whatever You Resolve to Be": Essays on Stonewall Jackson.*

ROBERT K. KRICK grew up in California but has lived and worked on the Virginia battlefields for twenty years. He is the author of dozens of articles and nine books, the most recent being *Stonewall Jackson at Cedar Mountain*, a selection of the History Book Club.

ALAN T. NOLAN, an Indianapolis lawyer, is a graduate of Indiana University and the Harvard Law School. He is Chairman of the Board of Trustees of the Indiana Historical Society and a member of the Indianapolis Civil War Round Table. In addition to articles in Civil War periodicals, he is the author of *The Iron Brigade: A Military History* and *Lee Considered: General Robert E. Lee and Civil War History.*